P9-APR-977

COMMUNITAS

Means of Livelihood and Ways of Life

COMMUNITAS

Means of Livelihood
and Ways of Life

Percival *and* Paul
Goodman

Preface
by Paul Goldberger

Afterword: Communitas Revisited
by Percival Goodman

Columbia University Press
A Morningside Book

Columbia University Press Morningside Edition
Columbia University Press
New York   Oxford
© Copyright, 1947, 1960, by Percival and Paul Goodman
Copyright © by the Estates of Percival Goodman
and Paul Goodman
Library of Congress Catalog Card Number: 60-6381
Reprinted by arrangement with the Estates of
Percival Goodman and Paul Goodman

All rights reserved

Library of Congress Cataloging-in-Publication Data

Goodman, Percival.
Communitas : means of livelihood and ways of life / Percival and
Paul Goodman ; preface by Paul Goldberger ; afterword, Communitas
revisited by Percival Goodman.
p.   cm.
Reprint. Originally published: New York : Vintage Books, 1960.
"A Morningside book."
ISBN 0-231-07298-8. — ISBN 0-231-07299-6 (pbk.)
1. City planning.   2. Utopias.   I. Goodman, Paul, 1911–1972.
II. Title.
HT166.G637   1990
711'.4—dc20   90-1735
CIP

Morningside Edition 1990

Casebound editions of Columbia University Press books are
Smythsewn and printed on permanent and durable acid-free paper

Printed in the U.S.A.

c 10 9 8 7 6 5 4 3 2 1
p 10 9 8 7 6 5 4 3 2

CONTENTS

Preface

Paul Goldberger

Utopianism has gotten a bad name in the last generation, and for good reason: most utopian plans for cities are far-fetched and silly, not only impractical but dangerous. The idealized visions of the city put forth by most utopian planners of modern times, from Ebenezer Howard to Le Corbusier, from Frank Lloyd Wright to Paolo Soleri, have been Procrustean beds, forcing reality into preconceived forms that bear little relation to cities—or to human societies—as they truly are. It should come as no surprise, then, that the prevailing mood of the last twenty years has been to move in the opposite direction, away from utopianism, toward a more modest, pragmatic, and accepting view of how cities and communities should be formed. A generation shaken by the arrogance of most of the utopian urban planners of the 20th century—and brought up on the alternative intellectual diet of Jane Jacobs, Herbert Gans, Robert Venturi and Denise Scott Brown—is not inclined to think much of ideal solutions.

But if this more modest sensibility of our time contains wisdom, it is not without dangers of its own. It is easy today to be too accepting of what is, too willing to believe that the various forces acting upon the city will in and of themselves be able to reach a satisfactory kind of balance, and that he who plans least plans best. We have come all too often to assume that, like Adam Smith's invisible hand trusted to guide the workings of the free marketplace, there is an invisible force that will guarantee that the various interests at play in

the making of cities will somehow achieve an equitable de-
tente. And while these interests *are* aligned in a different way
than they were a generation ago—in nearly every community
of any size there is surely more power on the local level to
stop huge projects than there was twenty years ago, for example—the very strength of the political and economic forces
acting upon cities today tells us that something other than
laissez faire is at work. Cities do not occur purely by the hap-
penstance of the political process, and to believe that they do
is to risk complacency at best, and utter cynicism at worst.

Is it possible to be critical of today's complacency without
being as naive as the utopians of an earlier generation—to
believe that there is a value to ideal plans without being taken
in by ideologies so rigid, by worldviews so narrow, as to ig-
nore the complex and contradictory realities that cities inevitably possess? I think that it is, and that Paul and Percival
Goodman did precisely that in *Communitas*. The first edition
of this book was written more than 40 years ago, just before
modernist utopianism began to fade, and it possesses a welcome dash of realism. Indeed, some of its best passages are
the lengthy critiques of the utopian thinkers who preceded
the Goodmans; these sections stand as proof that Paul and
Percival Goodman were not taken in by any of the 20th century's great urban mythmakers, and in fact managed to produce some of the first cogent critical analyses of just why their
plans made no real sense at all. These sections look better
and better over time, for they remind us that at its best, this
book not only extended and reiterated the modern age's commitment to utopian thinking, but it also prefigured the criti-
cisms of utopia's most articulate critics. It was no small ac-
complishment to be able at once to underscore this century's
tradition of utopianism and to set the agenda for utopianism's
best critics.

The Goodmans' comments on garden cities, on Le Corbusier and on that tremendous force who ultimately influenced
20th-century cities more than any other, Robert Moses, are
equally damning. They dismiss garden cities with a wave of

the hand: "Rather than live in a garden city, an intellectual would rather meet a bear in the woods." They correctly praise Le Corbusier's foresight in envisioning that the city of the future would be technocratic and service-oriented—an observation that the 80's often believe had never been made before—but they conclude by noting that "The great machine of the Ville Radieuse, for all its constructivist beauty, is not a city at all." Exactly right, of course: Le Corbusier's vision of a city of sleek slabs standing in open space was primarily an esthetic dream, for all it pretended to being a complete social and political system. The Ville Radieuse is, at bottom, cold, anti-urban, and viciously simplistic, and while it was never built in literal form, its esthetic vision formed the basis for most postwar urban renewal in this country and abroad. So we have come to pay dearly for Le Corbusier's excessively simple view of urban form, and the Goodmans realized it first.

It is easy now to see the vast damage that the automobile has wrought on the American landscape; it was not so easy to see that in 1947, when the Goodmans not only noted critically that both Le Corbusier and Frank Lloyd Wright, in their otherwise entirely different utopian cities, had planned primarily for easy accommodation to the automobile, but also that Robert Moses's impact on the city was mainly automobile-oriented. "He has done our city of New York a disastrous disservice, in the interests of a special class," they wrote of Moses's elaborate parkway system stretching out into the New York suburbs. "Imagine if this expenditure had been more equitably divided to improve the center and make livable neighborhoods. . . . The general outlook of these rich, parkway-served counties is that of ignorant, smug parasites."

Daring words indeed in 1947, and prescient. So, too, with the praise for Camillo Sitte, the urban theorist whose writings on the design of city squares they hail as representing the search for a true urban esthetic. They are right, though few others saw Sitte's mission as clearly as they did back then, and in this we see that the Goodmans' priorities really are those of cities. Unlike urbanists of today they believe that there is a solution, that there is an ideal urban form—but unlike most of the previous utopians they want that form to be truly *urban*, to be full of density and energy and excitement, to be noble and civic and monumental and public in the greatest sense of all of these words.

It is difficult to be quite so enthusiastic about the actual plans the Goodmans propose—like all utopian city planners, they put great stock in the creation of a rational physical form, an overall pattern, for the city. What else, after all, is the utopian physical planner to do? But it is important to look beyond our age's prejudice against excessively formal and patterned physical plans and examine the value system beneath the Goodman plans. They turn out to be based not on the purist abstractions of most 20th-century utopian urban plans, but on a deeper, broader, more humanistic set of goals. The first scheme, "The Metropolis as a Department Store," by this phrase alone aligns itself with a different value system— one envisioning the city not as a place that closes off options, as most rigid physical plans do, but as a place that opens them up. It is a defense of the city as a marketplace, as a source of choice above all, and in this sense it seems far more topical.

The chapters outlining the ideal communities are rich in splendid observations, many of which foreshadow issues that have become all the more urgent today. The Goodmans are deeply concerned over the excessive separation between the home and the workplace, for example, which they see not only as a physical problem but also as a social and emotional one. The rise of mass communications, the age of computers and fax machines, has made the importance they give to this issue all the more contemporary. So, too, with their suggestion that great works of art be dispersed from museums and distributed to individual communities—it is not about to happen, obviously, but it brings to the fore a concern about the role that art in the public place should have that remains critical today. And their preoccupation with breaking down the vast city into livable neighborhood units reminds us that they are not, in the end, as far away as they might seem from many of the last generation's post-utopian thinkers.

Ultimately, the great contribution this book made 42 years ago—and continues to make today—is not in the specifics of its plans at all, but in the eloquence and determination with which it testifies to the notion that the architect's mission is a broad one: that he or she is not merely a maker of shapes, but a force for social good. *Communitas* stands today as a rebuke to the indifference with which our current age views social responsibility, as a response to the tendency of our age to elevate the private realm above all. Paul and Percival Goodman believed with passion in the public realm, in the notion that there are public places, public ideas, public duties and responsibilities, that transcend the private and narrow concerns of individuals. *Communitas* is a testament to the idea that the city is a collective, shared place, a place that is in the most literal sense common ground. It emerges from the belief that the architect has an ability, not to mention a duty, to exercise vision, to dream of better ways of doing things and not merely to respond to the narrow demands of the moment. More than anything else, Paul and Percival Goodman in *Communitas* gave respectability to the business of being a visionary. The Goodmans' vision only begins with improving the city as a physical entity—its real goal is to elevate the very idea of the public realm, and make it noble once again.

COMMUNITAS

Means of Livelihood and Ways of Life

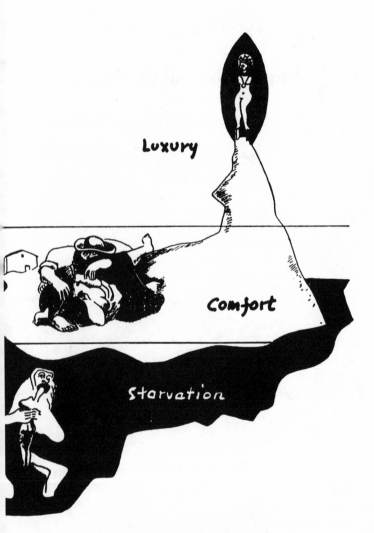

Luxury

Comfort

Starvation

Poverty, plenty and luxury

CHAPTER 1

Introduction

Background and Foreground

Of the man-made things, the works of engineering and architecture and town plan are the heaviest and biggest part of what we experience. They lie underneath, they loom around, as the prepared place of our activity. Economically, they have the greatest amount of past human labor frozen into them, as streets and highways, houses and bridges, and physical plant. Against this background we do our work and strive toward our ideals, or just live out our habits; yet because it is background, it tends to become taken for granted and to be unnoticed. A child accepts the man-made background itself as the inevitable nature of things; he does not realize that somebody once drew some lines on a piece of paper who might have drawn otherwise. But now, as engineer and architect once drew, people have to walk and live.

The background of the physical plant and the foreground of human activity are profoundly and intimately dependent on one another. Laymen do not realize how deep and subtle this connection is. Let us immediately give a strong architectural example to illustrate it. In Christian history, there is a relation between the theology and the architecture of churches. The dimly-lit vast auditorium of a Gothic Catholic cathedral, bathed in colors and symbols, faces a bright candle-lit stage and its richly costumed celebrant: this is the necessary background for the mysterious sacrament of the mass for the newly growing Medieval town and its representative actor. But the daylit, small, and unadorned meeting hall of the Congregationalist, facing its central pulpit, fits the belief that the chief mystery is preaching the

3

Word to a group that religiously governs itself. And the little square seating arrangement of the Quakers confronting one another is an environment where it is hoped that, when people are gathered in meditation, the Spirit itself will descend anew. In this sequence of three plans, there is a whole history of dogma and society. Men have fought wars and shed their blood for these details of plan and decoration.

Just so, if we look at the town plan of New Delhi we can immediately read off much of the history and social values of a late date of British imperialism. And if we look at the Garden City plan of Greenbelt, Md., we can understand something very important about our present American era of the "organization man."

We can read immediately from the industrial map of the United States in 1850 that there were sectional political interests. Given a certain kind of agricultural or mining plan, we know that, whatever the formal schooling of the society

Reading the social values from the plan: 1. New Delhi: British imperialism in India 2. Greenbelt, Md.: the disconnection of domestic and productive life

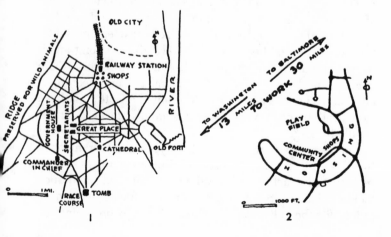

may be, a large part of the environmental education of the children will be technological; whereas a child brought up in a modern suburb or city may not even know what work it is that papa does "at the office."

Contemporary Criticism of Our American Way of Life

For thirty years now, our American way of life as a whole has been subjected to sweeping condemnation by thoughtful social and cultural critics. From the great Depression to World War II, this criticism was aimed mostly at our economic and political institutions; since the war, it has been aimed, less trenchantly but more broadly, at the Standard of Living, the popular culture, the ways of work and leisure. The critics have shown with pretty plain evidence that we spend our money for follies, that our leisure does not revive us, that our conditions of work are unmanly and our beautiful American classlessness is degenerating into a static bureaucracy; our mass arts are beneath contempt; our prosperity breeds insecurity; our system of distribution has become huckstering and our system of production discourages enterprise and sabotages invention.

In this book we must add, alas, to the subjects of this cultural criticism the physical plant and the town and regional plans in which we have been living so unsatisfactorily. We will criticize not merely the foolish shape and power of the cars but the cars themselves, and not merely the cars but the factories where they are made, the highways on which they run, and the plan of livelihood that makes those highways necessary. In appraising these things, we employ both the economic analysis that marked the books of the 30's and the socio-psychological approach prevalent since the war. This is indicated by our sub-title: "The Means of Livelihood and the Ways of Life." (In social theory, this kind of analysis provides one necessary middle term in the recent literature of criticism, between the economic and the cultural analyses, which have usually run strangely parallel to one another without touching.)

Nevertheless, except for this introductory chapter, this present book is *not* an indictment of the American way of life, but rather an attempt to clarify it and find what its possibilities are. For it is confused, it is a mixture of conflicting motives not ungenerous in themselves. Confronted with the spectacular folly of our people, one is struck not by their incurable stupidity but by their bafflement about what to do with themselves and their productivity. They seem to be trapped in their present pattern, with no recourse but to complicate present evils by more of the same. Especially in the field of big physical planning, there has been almost a total drying-up of invention, of new solutions. Most of the ideas discussed in this book come from the 20's or before, a few from the early 30's. Since World War II, with all the need for housing, with all the productive plant to be put to new work and capital to invest, the major innovation in community planning in the United States has been the out-of-town so-called "community center" whose chief structure is a supermarket where Sunday shoppers can avoid blue laws.

Typical American behavior is to solve a problem of transit congestion by creating a parallel system that builds up new neighborhoods and redoubles the transit congestion; but no effort is made to analyze the kinds and conditions of work so that people commute less. With generous intent, Americans clear a slum area and rebuild with large projects that re-create the slum more densely and, on the whole, sociologically worse, for now class stratification is built organically into the plan; but rarely is an effort made to get people to improve what they have, or to find out where they ought to move. (The exceptions—of the Hudson Guild in New York teaching six Puerto Rican families to make furniture and paint the premises, or of a block getting together to plant nine trees—are so exceptional that they warrant medals from the American Institute of Architects.) A classical example of our present genius in planning is solving the traffic jam on the streets of a great city in the West by making a system of freeways so fast and efficient with its cloverleaves as to occupy 40% of the real estate, whose previous occupants then move to distant places and drive back bumper-to-bumper on the freeways.

If, however, someone plans in a physicianly way to remedy the causes of an ill rather than concentrate on the symptoms, if he proposes a Master Plan to provide for orderly future development, if he suggests an inventive new solution altogether, then he is sure to be called impractical, irresponsible, and perhaps a subversive alien. Indeed, in the elegant phrase of the famous Park Commissioner of an Eastern metropolis, a guardian of the public welfare and morals in the field, such people are *Bei-unskis*, that is, Russian or German refugees who say, "*Bei uns* we did it this way."

Inherent Difficulties of Planning

Yet even apart from public foolishness and public officials, big physical planning is confusing and difficult. Every community plan is based on some:

> Technology
> Standard of Living
> Political and Economic Decision
> Geography and History of a Place.

Every part of this is thorny and the interrelation is thorny.

There may be historical miscalculation—wrong predictions in the most expensive matters. Consider, for instance, a most celebrated example of American planning, the laying-out of the District of Columbia and the city of Washington. When the site on the Potomac was chosen, as central in an era of slow transportation, the plan was at the same time to connect the Potomac waterway with the Ohio, and the new city was then to become the emporium of the West.

But the system of canals which would have realized this ambitious scheme did not materialize, and therefore, a hundred years later, Washington was still a small political center, pompously overplanned, without economic significance, while the commerce of the West flowed through the Erie Canal to New York. Yet now, ironically enough, the political change to a highly centralized bureaucracy has made Washington a great city far beyond its once exaggerated size.

Planners tend to put a misplaced faith in some one important factor in isolation, usually a technological innovation. In 1915, Patrick Geddes argued that, with the change from coal to electricity, the new engineering would, or could, bring into being Garden Cities everywhere to replace the slums; for the new power could be decentralized and was not in itself offensive. Yet the old slum towns have largely passed away to be replaced by endless conurbations of suburbs smothered in new feats of the new engineering— and the automobile exhaust is more of a menace than the coal smoke. Our guess is that these days nucleonics as such will not accomplish miracles for us, nor even automation.

The Garden City idea itself, as we shall see in the next chapter, has had a pathetic history. When Ebenezer Howard thought it up to remedy the coal slums, he did not contemplate Garden Cities without industry; he wanted to make it possible for people to live decently *with* the industry. Yet, just when the conditions of manufacture have become less noisome, it has worked out that the Green Belt and Garden Cities have become mere dormitories for commuters, who are also generally *not* the factory workers whom Howard had in mind.

Political Difficulties

The big, heavy, and expensive physical environment has always been the chief locus of vested rights stubbornly opposing planning innovations that are merely for the general

Washington's proposal to connect the Potomac and Ohio rivers

welfare and do not yield quick profits. A small zoning ordinance is difficult to enact, not to speak of a master plan for progressive realization over twenty or thirty years, for zoning nullifies speculation in real estate. Every advertiser in *American City* and *Architectural Forum* has costly wares to peddle, and it is hard to see through their smokescreen what services and gadgets are really useful, and whether or not some simpler, more inexpensive arrangement is feasible. Since streets and subways are too bulky for the profits of capricious fads, the tendency of business in these lines is to repeat the tried and true, in a bigger way. And it happens to be just the real estate interests and great financiers like insurance companies who have influence on city councils and park commissioners.

But also, apart from business interests and vested rights, common people are rightly very conservative about changes in the land, for they are very powerfully affected by such

changes in very many habits and sentiments. Any community plan involves a formidable choice and fixing of living
standards and attitudes, of schedule, of personal and cultural tone. Generally people move in the existing plan unconsciously, as if it were nature (and they will continue
to do so, until suddenly the automobiles don't move at all).
But let a new proposal be made and it is astonishing how
people rally to the old arrangement. Even a powerful park
commissioner found the housewives and their perambu-
lators blocking his way when he tried to rent out a bit of
the green as a parking lot for a private restaurant he favored;
and wild painters and cat-keeping spinsters united to keep
him from forcing a driveway through lovely Washington
Square. These many years now since 1945, the citizens of
New York City have refused to say "Avenue of the Ameri-
cas" when they plainly mean Sixth Avenue.

The trouble with this good instinct—not to be regimented
in one's intimate affairs by architects, engineers, and international public-relations experts—is that "no plan" always
means in fact some inherited and frequently bad plan. For
our cities are far from nature, that has a most excellent plan,
and the "unplanned" tends to mean a gridiron laid out for
speculation a century ago, or a dilapidated downtown when
the actual downtown has moved uptown. People are right
to be conservative, but what *is* conservative? In planning,
as elsewhere in our society, we can observe the paradox that
the wildest anarchists are generally affirming the most
ancient values, of space, sun, and trees, and beauty, human
dignity, and forthright means, as if they lived in neolithic
times or the Middle Ages, whereas the so-called conserva-
tives are generally arguing for policies and prejudices that
date back only four administrations.

The best defense against planning—and people do need
a defense against planners—is to become informed about the
plan that is indeed existent and operating in our lives; and
to learn to take the initiative in proposing or supporting
reasoned changes. Such action is not only a defense but

good in itself, for to make positive decisions for one's community, rather than being regimented by others' decisions, is one of the noble acts of man.

Technology of Choice and Economy of Abundance

The most curious anomaly, however, is that modern technology baffles people and makes them timid of innovations in community planning. It is an anomaly because for the first time in history we have, spectacularly in the United States, a surplus technology, a technology of free choice, that allows for the most widely various community-arrangements and ways of life. Later in this book we will suggest some of the extreme varieties that are technically feasible. And with this technology of choice, we have an economy of abundance, a standard of living that is in many ways *too* high—goods and money that are literally thrown away or given away—that could underwrite sweeping reforms and pilot experiments. Yet our cultural climate and the state of ideas are such that our surplus, of means and wealth, leads only to extravagant repetitions of the "air-conditioned nightmare," as Henry Miller called it, a pattern of life that used to be unsatisfactory and now, by the extravagance, becomes absurd.

Think about a scarcity economy and a technology of necessity. A cursory glance at the big map will show what we have inherited from history. Of the seven urban areas of the United Kingdom, six coincide with the coal beds; the seventh, London, was the port open to the Lowlands and Europe. When as children we used to learn the capitals and chief cities of the United States, we learned the rivers and lakes that they were located on, and then, if we knew which rivers were navigable and which furnished waterpower, we had in a nutshell the history of American economy. Not long ago in this country many manufacturers moved south to get cheaper labor, until the labor unions followed them. In general, if we look at the big historical map, we see that the location of towns has depended on bringing together the raw material and the power, on minimizing transportation, on having a reserve of part-time and seasonal labor and a concentration of skills, and sometimes (depending on the bulk or perishability of the finished product) on the location of the market. These are the kinds of technical and economic factors that have historically determined, with an iron necessity, the big physical plan of industrial nations and continents.

They will continue to determine them, but the iron necessity is relaxed. For almost every item that men have invented or nature has bestowed, there are alternative choices. What used to be made of steel (iron ore and coal) may now often be made of aluminum (bauxite and waterpower) or even of plastic (soybeans and sunlight). Raw materials have proliferated, sources of power have become more ubiquitous, and there are more means of transportation and lighter loads to carry. With the machine-analysis of manufacture, the tasks of labor become simpler, and as the machines have become automatic our problem has become, astoundingly, not where to get labor but how to use leisure. Skill is no longer the arduously learned craftsmanship of hundreds of trades and crafts—for its chief habits (styling, accuracy, speed) are built into the machine; skill has come to mean skill in a few operations, like turning, grinding, stamping, welding, spraying and half a dozen others, that intelligent people can learn in a short time. Even inspection is progressively mechanized. The old craft-operations of building could be revolutionized overnight if there were worthwhile enterprises to warrant the change, that is, if there were a social impetus and enthusiasm to build what everybody agrees is useful and necessary.

Consider what this means for community planning on any scale. We could centralize or decentralize, concentrate population or scatter it. If we want to continue the trend away from the country, we can do that; but if we want to combine town and country values in an agrindustrial way of life, we can do that. In large areas of our operation, we could go back to old-fashioned domestic industry with perhaps even a gain in efficiency, for small power is everywhere available, small machines are cheap and ingenious, and there are easy means to collect machined parts and centrally assemble them. If we want to lay our emphasis on providing still more mass-produced goods, and raising the standard of living still higher, we can do that; or if we want to increase leisure and the artistic culture of the individual, we can do that. We can have solar machines for hermits in the desert like Aldous Huxley or central heating provided for millions by New York Steam. All this is commonplace; everybody knows it.

It is *just* this relaxing of necessity, this extraordinary flexibility and freedom of choice of our techniques, that is baffling and frightening to people. We say, "If we want, we can," but offered such wildly possible alternatives, how the devil would people know what they want? And if you ask them—as it was customary after the war to take polls and ask, "What kind of town do you want to live in? What do you want in your post-war home?"—the answers reveal a banality of ideas that is hair-raising, with neither rational thought nor real sentiment, the conceptions of routine and inertia rather than local patriotism or personal desire, of prejudice and advertising rather than practical experience and dream.

Technology is a sacred cow left strictly to (unknown) experts, as if the form of the industrial machine did not profoundly affect every person; and people are remarkably superstitious about it. They think that it is more efficient to centralize, whereas it is usually more inefficient. (When this same technological superstition invades such a sphere as the school system, it is no joke.) They imagine, as an article of faith, that big factories must be more efficient than small ones; it does not occur to them, for instance, that it is cheaper to haul machined parts than to transport workmen.

Indeed, they are outraged by the good-humored demonstrations of Borsodi that, in hours and minutes of labor, it is probably cheaper to grow and can your own tomatoes than to buy them at the supermarket, not to speak of the quality. Here once again we have the inevitable irony of history: industry, invention, scientific method have opened new opportunities, but just at the moment of opportunity, people have become ignorant by specialization and superstitious of science and technology, so that they no longer know what they want, nor do they dare to command it. The facts are exactly like the world of Kafka: a person has every kind of electrical appliance in his home, but he is balked, cold-fed, and even plunged into darkness because he no longer knows how to fix a faulty connection.

Certainly this abdication of practical competence is one important reason for the absurdity of the American Standard of Living. Where the user understands nothing and cannot evaluate his tools, you can sell him anything. It is the user, said Plato, who ought to be the judge of the chariot. Since he is not, he must abdicate to the values of engineers, who are craft-idiots, or—God save us!—to the values of salesmen. Insecure as to use and value, the buyer clings to the autistic security of conformity and emulation, and he can no longer dare to ask whether there is a relation between his Standard of Living and the satisfactoriness of life. Yet in a reasonable mood, nobody, but nobody, in America takes the American standard seriously. (This, by the way, is what Europeans don't understand; we are not such fools as they imagine—we are far more at a loss than they think.)

Still Another Obstacle

We must mention still another obstacle to community planning in our times and a cause of the dull and unadventurous thinking about it: the threat of war, especially atomic war. People feel—and they are bang right—that there is

TOWNSCAPE 196–?

1. Abandoned city, could serve as decoy 2. Factory 3. Rocket Launching Platform 4. Entrances to Factory 5. Road under 6. Dwellings 7. Landing field 8. Trojan horses 9. Staff meeting 10. G.H.Q.

not much point in initiating large-scale and long-range improvements in the physical environment, when we are uncertain about the existence of a physical environment the day after tomorrow. A sensible policy for highways must be sacrificed to the needs of moving defense. Nor is this defeated attitude toward planning relieved when military experts come forth with spine-tingling plans that propose the total disruption of our present arrangements solely in the interest of minimizing the damage of the bombs. Such schemes do not awaken enthusiasm for a new way of life.

But even worse than this actual doubt, grounded in objective danger, is the world-wide anxiety that everywhere produces conformity and brain washed citizens. For it takes

a certain basic confidence and hope to be able to be rebel-
lious and hanker after radical innovations. As the historians
point out, it is not when the affairs of society are at low ebb,
but on the upturn and in the burst of revival that great
revolutions occur. Now compare our decade since World
War II with the decade after World War I. In both there
was unheard of productivity and prosperity, a vast expansion in science and technique, a flood of international exchange. But the decade of the 20's had also one supreme
confidence, that there was never going to be another war;
the victors sank their warships in the sea and every nation
signed the Kellogg-Briand pact; and it was in that confidence that there flowered the Golden Age of avant-garde
art, and many of the elegant and audacious community
plans that we shall discuss in the following pages. Our
decade, alas, has had the contrary confidence—God grant
that we are equally deluded—and our avant-garde art and
thought have been pretty desperate.

The future is gloomy, and we offer you a book about the
bright face of the future! It is because we have a stubborn
faith in the following proposition: the chief, the underlying
reason that people wage war is that they do not wage peace.
How to wage peace?

The Importance of
Planning in Modern Thinking

There is an important sense in which physical community
planning as a major branch of thought belongs to modern
times, to the past hundred years. In every age there have
been moral and cultural crises—and social plans like the
Republic—and also physical plans to meet economic, ecological, or strategic needs. But formerly the physical plans
were simply technical solutions: the physical motions and
tangible objects of people were ready means to express
whatever values they had; moral and cultural integration
did not importantly depend on physical integration. In our

times, however, every student of the subject complains, one way or another, that the existing physical plant is *not* expressive of people's real values: it is "out of human scale," it is existentially "absurd," it is "paleo-technological." Put philosophically, there is a wrong relation between means and ends. The means are too unwieldy for us, so our ends are confused, for impracticable ends are confused dreams. Whatever the causes, from the earliest plans of the modern kind, seeking to remedy the evils of nuisance factories and urban congestion, and up to the most recent plans for regional development and physical science fiction, we find always the insistence that reintegration of the physical plan is an essential part of political, cultural, and moral reintegration. Most physical planners vastly overrate the importance of their subject; in social change it is not a primary motive. When people are personally happy it is astonishing how they make do with improbable means—and when they are miserable the shiniest plant does not work for them. Nevertheless, the plans discussed in this book will show, we think, that the subject is more important than urban renewal, or even than solving traffic jams.

Neo-Functionalism

Finally, let us say something about the esthetic standpoint of this book. The authors are both artists and, in the end, beauty is our criterion, even for community planning, which is pretty close to the art of life itself. Our standpoint is given by the historical situation we have just discussed: the problem for modern planners has been the disproportion of means and ends, and the beauty of community plan is the proportion of means and ends.

Most of modern architecture and engineering has advanced under the banner of functionalism, "form follows function." This formula of Louis Sullivan has been subject to two rather contrary interpretations. In Sullivan's original statement he seemed to mean not that the form grows from

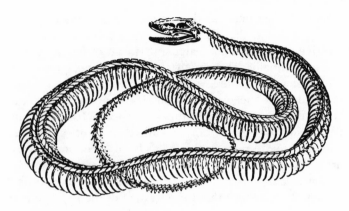

Constructivist functionalism

the function, but that it is appropriate to it, it is an interpretation of it; he says, "a store must look like a store, a bank must look like a bank." The formula aims at removing the ugliness of cultural dishonesty, snobbery, the shame of physical function. It is directly in the line of Ibsen, Zola, Dreiser. But it also affirms ideal forms, given by the sensibility of the culture or the imagination of the artist; and this is certainly how it was spectacularly applied by Sullivan's disciple, Frank Lloyd Wright, who found his shapes in America, in the prairie, and in his personal poetry.

In a more radical interpretation—e.g., of the Bauhaus— the formula means that the form is given by the function: there is to be no addition to the arrangement of the utility, the thing is presented just as it works. In a sense, this is not an esthetic principle at all, for a machine simply working perfectly would not be noticed at all and therefore would not have beauty nor any other sensible satisfaction. But these theorists were convinced that the natural handling of materials and the rationalization of design for mass production must necessarily result in strong elementary and intellectual satisfactions: simplicity, cleanliness, good sense, richness of texture. The bread-and-butter values of poor people who have been deprived, but know now what they want.

Along this path of interpretation, the final step seemed to be constructivism, the theory that since the greatest and most striking impression of any structure is made by its basic materials and the way they are put together, so the greatest formal effect is in the construction itself, in its clarity, ingenuity, rationality, and proportion. This is a doctrine of pure esthetics, directly in the line of post-impressionism, cubism, and abstract art. In architecture and engineering it developed from functionalism, but in theory and sometimes in practice it leaped to the opposite extreme of having no concern with utility whatever. Much constructivist architecture is best regarded primarily as vast abstract sculpture; the search of the artist is for new structural forms, arbitrarily, whatever the function. Often it wonderfully expresses the intoxication with new technology, how we can freely cantilever anything, span any space. On the other hand, losing the use, it loses the intimate sensibility of daily life, it loses the human scale.

We therefore, going back to Greek antiquity, propose a different line of interpretation altogether: form follows function, but let us subject the function itself to a formal critique. Is the *function* good? Bona fide? Is it worthwhile? Is it worthy of a man to do that? What are the consequences? Is it compatible with other, basic, human functions? Is it a forthright or at least ingenious part of life? Does it make sense? Is it a beautiful function of a beautiful power? We have grown unused to asking such ethical questions of our machines, our streets, our cars, our towns. But nothing less will give us an esthetics for community planning, the proportioning of means and ends. For a community is not a construction, a bold Utopian model; its chief part is always people, busy or idle, en masse or a few at a time. And the problem of community planning is not like arranging people for a play or a ballet, for there are no outside spectators, there are only actors; nor are they actors of a scenario but agents of their own needs—though it's a grand thing for us to be not altogether unconscious of forming a beautiful and elaborate city, by how we look and move. That's a proud feeling.

What we want is style. Style, power and grace. These come only, burning, from need and flowing feeling; and that fire brought to focus by viable character and habits.

This, then, is a book about the issues important in community planning and the ideas suggested by the planners. Our aim is to clarify a confused subject, to heighten the present low level of thinking; it is *not* to propose concrete plans for construction in particular places. We are going to discuss many big schemes, including a few of our own invention; but our purpose is a philosophical one: to ask what is socially implied in any such scheme as a way of life, and how each plan expresses some tendency of modern

The planner's ideal:
fitting the man to the plan

mankind. Naturally we too have an idea as to how *we* should like to live, but we are not going to try to sell it here. On the contrary! At present *any* plan will win our praise so long as it is really functional according to the criterion we have proposed: so long as it is aware of means and ends and is not, as a way of life, absurd.

A great plan maintains an independent attitude toward both the means of production and the standard of living. It is selective of current technology because how men work and make things is crucial to how they live. And it is selective of the available goods and services, in quantity and quality, and in deciding which ones are plain foolishness.

From the vast and curious literature of this subject during the past century, we have chosen a manual of great modern plans, and arranged them according to the following principle: What is the relationship between the arrangements for working and the arrangements for "living" (animal, domestic, avocational, and recreational)? What is the relation in the plan between production and consumption? This gives us a division into three classes:

A. *The Green Belt*—Garden Cities and Satellite Towns; City neighborhoods and the Ville Radieuse;
B. *Industrial Plans*—the Plan for Moscow; the Lineal City; Dymaxion;
C. *Integrated Plans*—Broadacres and the Homestead; the Marxist regional plan and collective farming; the T.V.A.

The first class, controlling the technology, concentrates on amenity of living; the second starts from arrangements for production and the use of technology; the third looks for some principle of symbiosis. It does not much matter whether we have chosen the most exciting or influential examples—though we have chosen good ones—for our aim is to bring out the principle of interrelation. Certainly we do not treat the plans in a way adequate to their merit, for they were put forth as practical or ideally practical schemes—

some of them were put into effect—whereas we are using them as examples for analysis.

The questions we shall be asking are: What do these plans envisage about:

> Kind of technology?
> Attitude toward the technology?
> Relation of work and leisure?
> Domestic life?
> Education of children and adults?
> Esthetics?
> Political initiative?
> Economic institutions?
> Practical realization?

By asking these questions of these modern plans, we can collect a large body of important issues and ideas for the inductions that we then draw in the second part of this book.

PART I

A Manual of Modern Plans

Difficulty of quarantining technology

CHAPTER 2

The Green Belt

The original impulse to Garden City planning was the reaction against the ugly technology and depressed humanity of the old English factory areas. On the one hand, the factory poured forth its smoke, blighted the countryside with its refuse, and sucked in labor at an early age. On the other, the homes were crowded among the chimneys as identical hives of labor power, and the people were parts of the machine, losing their dignity and sense of beauty. Some moralists, like Ruskin, Morris, and Wilde reacted so violently against the causes that they were willing to scrap both the technology and the profit system; they laid their emphasis on the beauty of domestic and social life, making for the most part a selection of pre-industrial values. Ruskin praised the handsome architecture of the Middle Ages, said things should not be made of iron, and campaigned for handsome tea cannisters. Morris designed furniture and textiles, improved typography, and dreamed of society without coercive law. Wilde (inspired also by Pater) tried to do something about clothing and politics and embarked on the so-called "esthetic adventure." What is significant is the effort to combine large-scale social protest with a new attitude toward small things.

Less radically, Ebenezer Howard, the pioneer of the Garden City, thought of the alternative of quarantining the technology, but preserving both the profit system and the copiousness of mass products: he protected the homes and the non-technical culture behind a belt of green. This idea caught on and has been continually influential ever since. In all Garden City planning one can detect the purpose of safeguard, of defense; but by the same token, this is the school that has made valuable studies of minimum living standards, optimum density, right orientation for sunlight, space for playgrounds, the correct designing of primary schools.

Plans which in principle quarantine the technology start with the consumption products of industry and plan for the amenity and convenience of domestic life. Then, however, by a reflex of their definition of what is intolerable and substandard, in domestic life, they plan for the convenience and amenity also of working conditions, and so they meet up with the stream of the labor movement.

With the coming of the automobiles there was a second impulse to Garden City planning. To the original ugliness of coal was added the chaos of traffic congestion and traffic hazard. But there was offered also the opportunity to get away faster and farther. The result has been that, whereas for Howard the protected homes were near the factories and planned in conjunction with them, the entities that are now called Garden Cities are physically isolated from their industry and planned quite independently. We have the interesting phenomena of commutation, highway culture, suburbanism, and exurbanism.

The chief property of these plans, then, is the setting-up of a protective green belt, and the chief difference among the plans depends on how complex a unity of life is provided off the main roads leading to the industrial or business center.

We are now entering a stage of reflex also to this second impulse of suburbanism: *not* to flee from the center but to open it out, relieve its congestion, and bring the green belt into the city itself. This, considered on a grand scale, is the proposal of the Ville Radieuse of Le Corbusier. Considered more piecemeal, it employs the principle of enclosed traffic-free blocks and the revival of neighborhoods, as proposed by disciples of Le Corbusier, like Paul Wiener, or housers like Henry Wright.

Suburban view

From Suburbs to Garden Cities

From the countryside, the scattered people crowd into cities and overcrowd them. There then begins a contrary motion.

Consider first the existing suburbs. These are unorganized settlements springing up on the main highway and parallel railway to the city. They take advantage of the cheaper land far from the center to build chiefly one-family houses with private yards. The productive and cultural activity of the

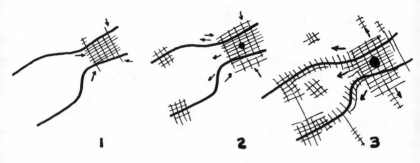

adults and even adolescents is centered in the metropolis; it is only the children who belong strictly to the suburb as such. The principal civic services—paving, light, water—are directed by the city; and the land is surveyed according to the prevailing city plan, probably in a grid. The highway to the city is the largest street and contains the shops.

Spaced throughout the grid are likely to be small developments of private real estate men, attempting a more picturesque arrangement of the plots. But on the whole the pressure for profit is such that the plots become minimal and the endless rows of little boxes, or of larger boxes with picture windows, are pretty near the landscape of Dante's first volume.

Such development is originally unplanned. It is best described in the phrase of Mackaye as "urban backflow." The effect of it is, within a short time, to reach out toward the next small or large town and to create a still greater and more planless metropolitan area. This is the ameboid spreading that Patrick Geddes called conurbation.

Culturally, the suburb is too city-bound to have any definite character, but certain tendencies are fairly apparent —caused partly by the physical facts and partly, no doubt, by the kind of persons who choose to be suburbanites. Families are isolated from the more diverse contacts of city culture, and they are atomized internally by the more frequent absence of the wage earner. On the other hand, there is a growth of neighborly contacts. Surburbanites are known

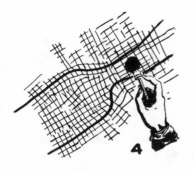

Conurbation (after Geddes):
1. Flow into the city
2. Inflow continues,
backflow to suburbs begins,
slums grow in the center
3. Backflow in full flood,
slums turn to blight
4. A sprawling mass with
a great central blighted area

as petty bourgeois in status and prejudice, and they have the petty bourgeois virtue of making a small private effort, with its responsibilities. There is increased dependency on the timetable and an organization of daily life probably tighter than in the city, but there is also the increased dignity of puttering in one's own house and maybe garden. (It has been said, however, that the majority dislike the gardening and keep up the lawn just to avoid unfavorable gossip.) There is no local political initiative, and in general politics there is a tendency to stand pat or retreat.

When this suburban backflow is subjected to conscious planning, however, a definite character promptly emerges. Accepting such a tendency as desirable, the city makes political and economic decisions to facilitate it by opening fast highways or rapid-transit systems from the center to the outskirts. An example is the way the New York region has been developed. The effect is to create blighted areas in the depopulated center, to accelerate conurbation at the periphery and rapidly depress the older suburbs, choking their traffic and destroying their green; but also to open out much further distances (an hour away on the new highways) where there is more space and more pretentious housing. This is quite strictly a middle-class development; for the highways draw heavily on the social wealth of everybody for the benefit of those who are better off, since the poor can afford neither the houses nor the automobiles.

This matter is important and let us dwell on it a moment.

A powerful Park Commissioner has made himself a vast
national reputation by constructing many such escape-highways: they are landscaped and have gas-stations in quaint
styles; this is "a man who gets things done." He has done
our city of New York a disastrous disservice, in the interests of a special class. Imagine if this expenditure had been
more equitably divided to improve the center and make
liveable neighborhoods, as was often suggested. The situation in the New York region is especially unjust. Those who
can afford to live in Nassau or Westchester Counties are able
to avoid also the city sales and other taxes, although para-
sitically they enjoy the city's culture; yet, having set up a
good swimming pool across the city's northern border, the
people of Westchester have indignantly banned its use to
Negroes, Puerto Ricans, and other poor kids since they
made it "for their own people." The general outlook of these
rich parkway-served counties is that of ignorant, smug
parasites.

A more rational inference from the suburban impulse is
the idea of the Ciudad Linéal (after Soria y Mata), proposed as long ago as 1882 for the development of the outskirts of Madrid. The Lineal City, continuous roadside
development, is the planned adaptation of existing "ribbon
development," the continuous dotting of habitations along
any road. It avoids the high rent and congestion of the city,
has easy access to the city, and it minimizes the invasion of
the forest and countryside, which begin immediately beyond the street off the highway. It is essentially a European
invention, for this is in fact the form of the villages of Italy,
France, Spain, or Ireland: row-housing on both sides of
the highroad, and the peasants' fields out the back door
(whereas the English and Americans have historically
spread over the fields with detached houses). The chief
importance of the Lineal City, however, is not residential
but industrial; it is the simplest analysis of the always present and always major factor of transportation (see later,
plan of the disurbanists, p. 71)—a remarkable invention to
have been made before the coming of the automobile.

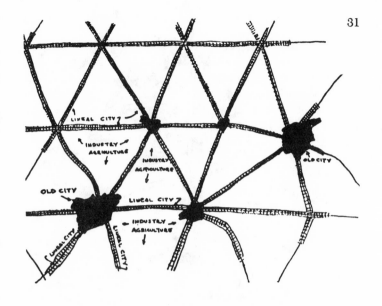

*Street and lineal plan of Ciudad Linéal
(after Soria y Mata)*

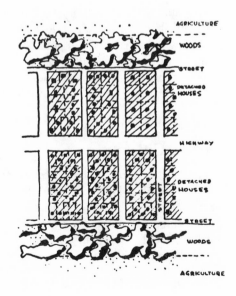

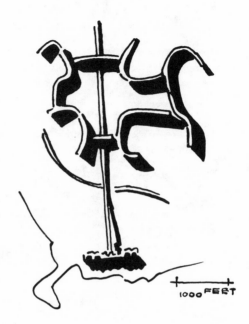

A modern proposal for a lineal city: Algiers, 1931 (Le Corbusier)

The climactic development of the suburban impulse in the English or American style is the Garden City in the form in which it is now laid out. This is a unified residential community of a size "sufficient for a complete social life," with row as well as detached houses, but mainly detached houses with small gardens, and with its center *off* the highway.

Garden Cities

The classic Garden City, Letchworth (architects: Parker and Unwin, after Howard), is a place of light industry. But let us here speak rather of places completely dependent on commuting, e.g., Radburn (Stein), Welwyn (Unwin), or the New Deal Greenbelt, Greendale, etc. Radburn aims at a population of 25,000. After 35 years, Letchworth numbered 17,000.

The following exposition is taken from the well-known book of Raymond Unwin, *Town Planning in Practice* (1907; rev. ed. 1932). He is concerned throughout with residential convenience and amenity. On industry his first and last word is, "We shall need power to reserve suitable areas for factories, where they will have every convenience for their work and cause the minimum of nuisance." One is struck by the expression *"their* work" rather than *"our* work."

Amenity. It is by adding amenity to physical convenience, says Unwin, that we get a Garden City. This curious British term, variously applied by every English planner, and imitated by the Americans, means decency, charm of appearance and privacy. To Unwin its first implication is zoning: segregation from industry and business, and the restriction of density to "twelve families to the acre"; further, it implies planning with an esthetic purpose.

Letchworth: the original Garden City

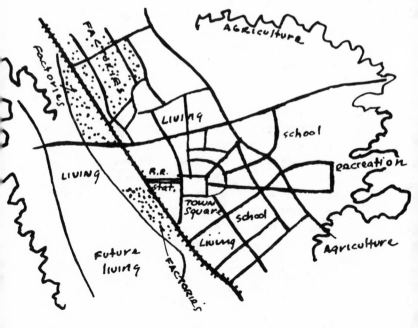

He proceeds to formal and informal plans, a distinction borrowed from English gardening. He himself prefers the formal or T-square and compass plan, obviously thinking of the delightful squares and crescents of London. (American designers, reacting to our undelightful gridirons, prefer ameboid shapes.) Next he speaks of problems of street-layout and the arrangement of public plazas. (American designers, faced with a heavy volume of through traffic, employ the cul-de-sac.) Next, the uniformity of materials for general effect. On this point, one is struck with the remembrance of the lovely uniformity of old French or Irish villages, a natural uniformity created by having to use local building materials; but in the Garden City we come to a situation of surplus means and planned uniformity to avoid chaos of the surplus. Next, Unwin cites the unity of design of the separate blocks of houses.

Unwin devotes his last chapter to an idea of great value: neighborly cooperation. Planning, he says, is cooperative in its essence. It starts with the location of the necessities of the community as a whole—its schools, shops, institutes. It modifies the individual or suburbanite taste to its plazas and prospects. It proposes the orientation and construction of houses. It suggests the summation of private gardens into orchards, and perhaps a common. By cooperation all can have "a share of the convenience of the rich . . . if we can overcome the excessive prejudice which shuts up each family and all its domestic activities within the precincts of its own cottage." He asks for the common laundry and nursery, common library, common services. "More difficult is the question of the common kitchen and dining hall." Indeed more difficult! For along this line of community commitment there opens up a new way of life altogether, with strong political consequences.

Unwin's book is admirably reasoned and well written; but how are the suburbanites of the beginning to become the fellowship of the end? Given the usual private or governmental projectors, unity of planning means sameness, and social landscaping means the restriction of children from climbing the trees like bad citizens. From the start he has isolated his community from the productive work of society. The initiative to cooperation does not rise from, nor reach toward, political initiative that always resides in the management of production and distribution. How far would that cooperation get?

What is the culture of Garden Cities? The community spirit belongs, evidently, to those who stay at home. As the suburb belongs to the children, here the community belongs to the children and some of the women. The women *are* neighborly; according to recent statistics, they spend ten hours a week playing cards and are active on committees. The men spend a good deal of the time on the prefabricated craftsmanship that we call "Do It Yourself." There is golf, for talking business or civil service. These are the topics of conversation because a lustier workman is not likely to divert so much of his time and income from the more thrilling excitements of the city, such as they are; and rather than live in a Garden City, an intellectual would rather meet a bear in the woods.

—caesio veniam
obvius leoni!

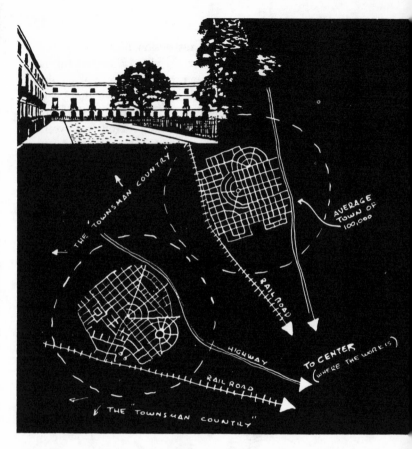

*A culture city. Above: Munster Square, London, a town style.
Below: regional plan according to Sharp's analysis*

Satellite Towns

To meet some of these objections the English planners
have invented Satellite Towns, in a serious effort to plan
for a culture full-blown rather than a week-end somnoles-
cence. To recover a true urbanism from the man-eating
megalopolis; and also to rescue from suburbia the countryside and the woods.

It seems to have been this latter purpose—the reaction to the fact that the spread-out Garden Cities encroach on the rural land—that has led the more recent generation of English planners, for example Thomas Sharp, to dissent from Howard. Whereas neither Howard nor Unwin has anything to say about the country as such, Sharp in his *Town Planning* devotes as much space to the amenity of the country as to the amenity of the town. Perhaps this reflects the great problem of an England stripped of its empire and needing to become more agriculturally self-sufficient.

(In America we have had the fine work of Mackaye, the creator of the Appalachian Trail. He is concerned to preserve the aboriginal woods as the vivifier of city life. Sharp too has a chapter on national parks for hikers and campers.)

Satellite towns are thought of as having a population of 100,000, where even Letchworth with its mills has less than 20,000. The "complete social life" of the Garden City is not a cultural life at all, for high culture is a defining property of cities. (A vast industrial concentration is not a city either, of course.)

More than any other plan the Satellite Town depends on belts of green, for the green must hem in not only the industrial center but also town from town, to protect the urban unity of each; and finally it must protect even the unity of the countryside.

A satellite town, then, is a true city economically dependent on a center and therefore on its highway, but laid out as if integral and self-sufficient. The ideal of the layout is taken directly from the squares and crescents of Christopher Wren and the Brothers Adam. The style proposed by Sharp is the "various monotony" of an eighteenth-century block, each of whose doorways and fan-windows is studied, the symbol that a man's home, not his house, is his castle. Country houses, too, have urban dignity, and the fields have humane hedgerows.

At its worst the culture of such a place would be exclusive and genteel, but at its best it would be the culture of little theaters. Now little theater is not amateurish, not the lawn pageant that belongs to the complete social life of Garden Cities; nor is it prefabricated "Do It Yourself"; nor again, of course, is it professional (and standardized) entertainment for broad masses. It is devoted to objective art, the use of the best modern means, and it cultivates its participants. Primary education would be progressive and independent, and higher education would teach the best that has been thought and said and study "monuments of its own magnificence." The countryside demonstrates how man can humanize nature and is a source of decent, not canned, food; and the national park revives us with the forthright causality of the woods. All conspires to the spiritual unity of the soul and the cultural unity of mankind (it is essential to the idea to mingle the economic classes)—all except the underlying work and techniques of society on which everything depends not only economically but in every big political decision and in the style of every object of use: these have no representation.

We are here in the full tide of cultural schizophrenia. When the suburbanite or Garden Citizen returns from the industrial center, it is with a physical release and a reawakening of cowering sensibilities. But the culture-townsman has raised his alienation to the level of a principle. What reintegration does he offer? The culture-townsman declares that we must distinguish ends and means, where industry is the means but town life is the end. Trained in his town to know what he is about, the young man can then turn to the proper ordering of society. In America this was fairly explicitly the program of Robert Hutchins. The only bother is that one cannot distinguish ends and means in this way and the attempt to do so emasculates the ends. Under these conditions, art is cultivated but no works of art can be made; science is studied but no new propositions are advanced; and living is central but there is no social invention. (But to be just, do we see any other communities that guarantee these excellent things?)

The form in which, at present, this plan is partly realized is the college campus and its neighborhood. It is a plan not for the children and women, but for the ephebes of both sexes and all ages. For the adults it is a conception appropriate to endowed rather than current wealth, and suspicious of change.

The Evolution of Streets from Village to City

We can tell the story of the inflow and backflow of a metropolitan population simply as a history of streets.

Starting new on Manhattan, in a territory from their point of view undeveloped, the Dutch first built a little town

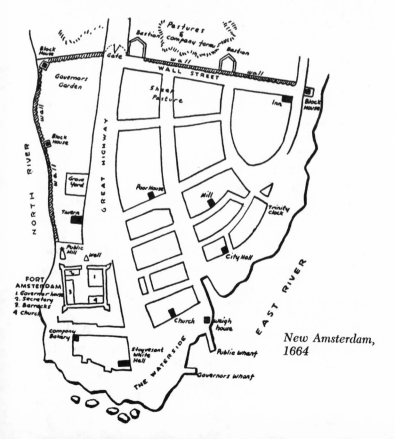

New Amsterdam, 1664

dependent on its own agriculture and on the commerce in
furs. Their square faced on the dock, it was the place of the
overseas market, of the imported government, and soon of
the community church and school. People lived on small
farms.

As the commerce grew and attracted greater numbers, the
original farms were subdivided for simple residence, and
the farmers, more ambitious because their products were
in demand both abroad and at home, took possession of
great domains throughout the island and northward. They
now found that the territory had already been somewhat
laid out by the aborigines, and they made use of the main
Indian trail, which to the Indians had run in the opposite
direction toward their capital at Dobbs Ferry. (The way
facing toward Europe was not so obviously downtown for
the Indians.) And it is striking how many features of the
aboriginal layout, topologically determined, persist in the
modern city, though the topology itself has been much
changed. The original lanes and highways of the Indians
and the patroon proprietors formed the basis of some of
the avenues of later days.

Very early some of the larger domains were subdivided
and occupied as villages of the growing town. The first
such was New Haarlem.

Finally, after the vicissitudes of the English occupation
and the American Revolution, it was clear that none of the
thriving commercial island would remain farm land, it
would all be subdivided for commerce, manufacture, and
residence. In 1807 almost the whole area was surveyed as
a gridiron, that lay across the aboriginal paths and the
early lanes and roads, unable to alter either the stronger
topological features or the areas already built up, but
dominating the future.

The rectangles of 1807 were subdivided by real estate
speculators into the lots and back alleys of 1907.

But when the subdivision was complete, began the backflow to the outskirts. Under the domination of the center,
these outskirts were surveyed in large rectangles and sold

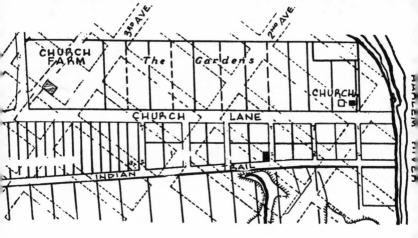

Village of New Haarlem, 1670, overlaid by 1811 gridiron

in small lots, for instance on Long Island. But since the impulse to suburban settlement is partly to escape the featureless and anonymous network, at least some of the rectangles have been arranged into "developments" with an artificial topology. This brings us back to the composite plan of 1807.

Let the impulse to escape continue, and a Garden City is laid out, off the main highway, deliberately demolishing the gridiron. It is a place of small gardens; the features of the topology again begin to appear; we are back to New Haarlem, except that the small gardens are not really small farms.

Lastly, in the ideal of a culture town, perhaps somewhere in Westchester or in Madison Avenue Connecticut, we return to the integrated town of 1640, built around its plaza. This plaza has perhaps a church, and perhaps a school, but no overseas market and no provincial governor. No farmers. No Indians.

And the plan after the last—is the city without streets. With the advent of the helicopter, this apparently anomalous conception will no doubt come to exist—it has already been suggested by Fuller and others.

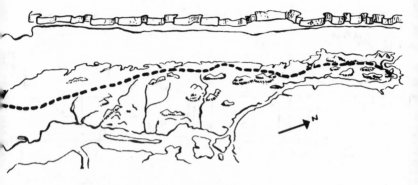

The Weckquaesgeck Trail in Manhattan (Broadway)

Another Version of the Same

Another way of looking at the same history of streets is to consider the steady growth of the old Weckquaesgeck Trail to become the Albany Post Road, then Broadway, then Route 9, and then the great Thruway.

The change to the Thruway is remarkable. For the first time the topological features are disregarded, and so, for the most part, are the settlements of population that are apparently served by the road. Instead, on these great superhighways we see developed a unique culture, with its own colors and eating habits, and a kind of extraterritorial law. Citizens of the Thruway, that stretches from coast to coast, must Go! Go! Not too fast and not too slow. Above all they must not stop. There are also new entities in pathology, such as driver's instep and falling asleep at the wheel.

Ville Radieuse

Let us now consider the contrary direction of green belt planning: to invade the center with green and set up Garden Cities in the megalopolis itself. Such a conception involves, of course, immense demolition, it is a surgical operation. And naturally, for such a "cartesian" solution, we must turn to the Ville Radieuse of Le Corbusier, a

Frenchman (he is even a Swiss!). For Paris is the only vast city with beauty *imposed* on her; and Baron Hausmann long ago showed that you must knock down a great deal to get a great result.

"To de-congest the centers—to augment their density—to increase the means of getting about--to increase the parks and open spaces": these are the principles of the Ville Radieuse. The plan is extremely simple and elegant: either demolish the existing chaos or start afresh on a new site; lay out in levels highways and tramways radiating from the center; on these erect a few towering skyscrapers every 400 meters at the subway stations; and ring this new opened-out center with large apartment houses for residences, a *Cité Jardin*, the French kind of Garden City. Industry will be quarantined somewhere "on the outskirts." (To Paris, Le Corbusier applied this scheme as the Voisin Plan; in the plan for Algiers, he replaced the residential rings by lineal cities.)

Similar solutions, one judged practical, one impractical: 1. Radio City in New York 2. Le Corbusier's Voisin project for Paris

1   2

This is a prince of plans. It is a typical flower of the twenties, of the Paris International Style. Its daring practicality seems to rejoice in the high capitalism of the "captains of industry," as Le Corbusier calls them, whose technology and financial resources can accomplish anything. We can see its shapes in Rio and Caracas and, grotesquely misapplied, in New York's Radio City.

In the central skyscrapers, says the author, are housed the brains and eyes of society. Wherever industry may be located "on the outskirts," its financial, technical, and political control is in these few towers. Ville Radieuse is a paper city; its activity is the motion of draftsmen, typists, accountants, and meetings of the board. Carried on in an atmosphere of conditioned air, corrected light, and bright décor, by electrical communications, with efficiency and speed. "The city that can achieve speed will achieve success. Work is today more intense and carried on at a quicker rate. The whole question becomes one of daily intercommunication with a view to settling the state of the market and the condition of labor. The more rapid the intercommunication, the more will business be expedited." Had this ever before been so succinctly stated? The passage was written by an architect before the coming of the giant computers and before we had learned to use the magic words "cybernetics" and "feedback."

Leaving the diffused center, we come to the rings of residence. The inner rings are commodious apartments for the wealthy, innermost like the first tiers at the opera. The outer rings are super-blocks of housing for the average, who travel either inward to the skyscrapers or outward, past the agricultural belt, to the factories.

The residences, great or small, are *machines à vivre,* machines for living, just as the skyscrapers are machines for communications and exchange, and the streets are machines for traffic. The plan extends inside the walls of the houses to the fittings and furniture. (Contrast this with the English Garden City planners who do not invade these private pre-

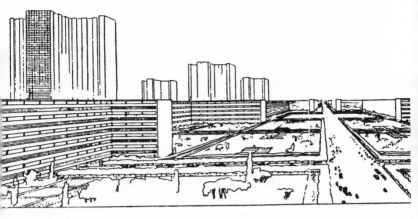

Residential zone, business center at left (after Le Corbusier)

cincts.) The unit of living is the cell (*céllule*), standard in construction and layout and arranged for mass servicing. Its furniture, too, is standardized, so that it doesn't matter in which cell a person lives, "for labor will shift about as needed and must be ready to move, bag and baggage." The standards are analyzed, however, not only for efficiency but for beauty and amenity—though, in this gipsy economy, domestic amenity is not the fundamental consideration. An outside room or "hanging garden" is provided in the smallest flat. It is a *Cité Jardin:* the ratio of empty space is large, and there are fields for outdoor sports right at the doorstep, if one had a doorstep.

"There must never come a time," says our author ominously, "when people can be bored in our city . . . In general we feel free in our own cell, and reality teaches us that the grouping of cells attacks our freedom, so we dream of a detached house. But it is possible, by a logical ordering of these cells, to attain freedom through order."

Being standard, every part is capable of mass production. In the English plans, even where the aim was urban uniformity, this was not thought of as mass produced. The manner of construction, like the ideal of small cooperatives, was proper to craft unions. But Le Corbusier, planning for the captains of industry, has only contempt for the mason who "bangs away with feet and hammer."

Esthetic interest is given by the variety of the grand divisions, seen at large and in long views, the skyscrapers towering on the horizon above the dwellings. "The determining factor in our feelings is the silhouette against the sky." And we can take advantage of the grand social divisions of rich and poor to give the variety of the sumptuous apartments with their set-back teeth (!—the word is *redents*) as against the rectangles of the workers' blocks.

The esthetic ideal is the geometric ordering of space, in prisms, straight lines, circles. It is the Beaux Arts' ideal of the symmetrical plan. The basis of beautiful order is the modulus, whose combinations are countable, so that we should have to simulate mass production even if technical efficiency did not demand it. Space is treated as an undifferentiated whole to be structured: we must avoid topological particularity and build always on a level. (If the site is not level, make a platform on pilotis.) The profile against the sky is the chief ordering of space and the prime determinant of feeling. Space flows inside and outside the buildings; we must use a lot of glass and lay the construction bare. And to insure the clarity and salience of the construction it is best to emphasize a single material, reinforced concrete, and it is even advisable to paint over the surfaces in a single color.

What shall we make of this? In this International Style —of Le Corbusier, Gropius, Oud, Neutra, Mies van der Rohe—there are principles that are imperishable: the analysis of functions, clarity of construction, emphasis on the plan, simplicity of surfaces, reliance on proportion, broad social outlook (whatever the kind of social outlook). It is the best of the Beaux Arts' tradition revivified and made profound by the politics and sociology of all the years since the fall of Louis XVI.

Yet in this version of Le Corbusier, the Ville Radieuse was the perfecting of a status quo, 1925, that as an ideal has al-

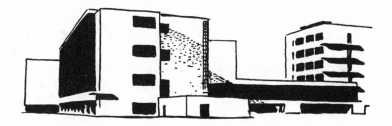

School (Gropius)

Home (Le Corbusier)

Exhibition Building (Mies van der Rohe)

ready perished—it died with the great Depression—though as a boring and cumbersome fact it is still coming into being: society as an Organization. Le Corbusier was a poor social critic and a bad prophet. He gets an esthetic effect from a distinction of classes and a spectacular expression of this distinction just when the wealthy class was about to assume a protective camouflage, and indeed just when it was plunging into the same popular movie-culture as everybody else and ceased to stand for anything at all. The brains and eyes of society he calls "captains of industry," but their function was to study the market and exploit labor; they were financiers. It was to these captains that he pathetically turned for the realization of his plan; he proposed that international capital invest in the rebuilding of Paris—the increase in land values would give them a quick profit— "and," he exclaimed, "this will stave off the war, because who would bomb the property in which he has an investment?" As it turned out, the unreconstructed Paris was *not* bombed.

His attitude toward technology is profoundly contradictory. Superficially, the Ville Radieuse makes use of the most advanced means; even the home is a machine. But he suggests nothing but the rationalization of existing means for greater profits in an arena of competition, saying, "The city that can achieve speed will achieve success." His aim is neither to increase productivity as an economist, nor, by studying the machines and their processes as a technologist, to improve them. Contrast his attitude with that of a technological planner like Buckminster Fuller, who finds in the machinery, for better or worse, a new code of values. Fuller is looking ahead of the technology to new inventions and new patterns of life; Le Corbusier is committed, by perfecting a status quo, to a maximum of inflexibility.

Caught in this Organization, what is the plight of the average man in the Ville Radieuse? The Garden Cities, we saw, were based on the humane intuition that work in which people have the satisfaction neither of direction nor craftsmanship, but merely of wages, is essentially unbearable; the worker is eager to be let loose and go far away, he must be protected by a green belt. (There are surveys that show that people do *not* want to live conveniently near their jobs!) Le Corbusier imagines, on the contrary, that by the negative device of removing bad physical conditions, people can be brought to a positive enthusiasm for their jobs. He is haunted by the thought of the likelihood of boredom, but he puts his faith in freedom through order. The order is apparent; what is the content of the freedom? Apart from a pecular emphasis on athletic sports and their superiority to calisthenics (!), this planner has nothing, but nothing, to say about education, sexuality, entertainment, festivals, politics. Meantime, his citizens are to behold everywhere, in the hugest and clearest expression in reinforced concrete and glass, the fact that their orderly freedom will last forever. It has 500 foot prisms in profile against the sky.

Le Corbusier wages a furious polemic against Camillo Sitte, author of *Der Städtebau,* who is obviously his bad conscience. He makes Sitte appear as the champion of picturesque scenery and winding roads. But in fact the noble little book of the scholarly Austrian is a theory of plazas, of city-squares; it attempts to answer the question, What is an *urban* esthetic? For in the end, the great machine of the Ville Radieuse, with all its constructivist beauty, is not a city at all.

City Squares

A city is made by the social congregation of people, for business and pleasure and ceremony, different from shop or office or private affairs at home. A person is a citizen in the street. A city street is not, as Le Corbusier thinks, a machine for traffic to pass through but a square for people to remain within. Without such squares—markets, cathedral places, political forums—planned more or less as inclosures, there is no city. This is what Sitte is saying. The city esthetic

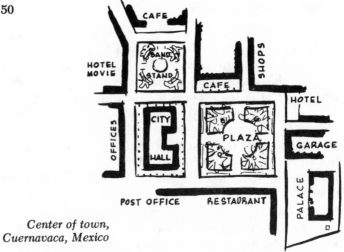

Center of town,
Cuernavaca, Mexico

is the beauty proper to being in or entering such a square; it consists in the right choice and disposition of structures in and around the square, and in the relation of the squares to one another. This was the Greek, medieval, or Renaissance fact of city life. A Greek, if free and male, was a city man, not a family man or an Organization man; he spent his time on the street, in the law court, at the market.

It is possible that this urban beauty is a thing of the past. Perhaps there are no longer real occasions for social congregation in the square. The larger transactions of business occur at a distance by "communication," not face to face. Politics is by press, radio, and ballot. Social pleasure is housed in theaters and dance halls. If this is so, it is a grievous and irreparable loss. There is no substitute for the spontaneous social conflux whose atoms unite, precisely, as citizens of the city. If it is so, our city crowds are doomed to be lonely crowds, bored crowds, humanly uncultured crowds.

Urban beauty does not require trees and parks. Classically, as Christopher Tunnard has pointed out, if the cities were small there were no trees. The urban use of trees is formal, like the use of water in fountains; it is to line a street or square, to make a cool spot, or a promenade like the miraculous Stephen's Green in Dublin. The Bois in Paris is a kind of picnic-ground for the Parisians, it is not a green belt. But when we come to the park systems of London, New York, or Chicago we already have proper green belts whose aim is to prevent a conurbation that would be stifling. (The effect in London and Chicago, of course, is that those cities stretch on and on and it is hard to get from one district to another.) And when finally, as in the Ville Radieuse, the aim is to make a city *in* the park, a Garden City, one has despaired of city life altogether.

Again, the urban beauty is a beauty of walking; and perhaps it has no place in the age of automobiles and airplanes. This raises the crucial question of standpoint, the point of view, in modern architectural esthetics. Again and again Le Corbusier proves that a place is ugly by showing us the view of the worm-heap from an airplane. Yet then, even the Piazza San Marco or the Piazza dei Signori, in Florence, which he cannot help but admire, merge indistinguishably

The Piazzetta, Venice

into the worm-heap. Indeed, from a moving airplane even the Ville Radieuse or New York aflame in the night lasts only a few minutes.

If the means of locomotion is walking, the devices described by Sitte—inclosure of streets, placing of a statue—can have a powerful architectural effect. If the means is the automobile, there is still place for architectural beauty, but it will reside mainly in the banking of roads, the landscaping, and the profile on the horizon. When our point of view is the airplane, however, the resources of architecture are helpless; nothing can impress us but the towering Alps, the towering clouds, or the shoreline of the sea.

The problem, the choice of the means of locomotion, is an important one. For not only Le Corbusier, who has a penchant for the grandiose, but also his opposite number in so many respects, Frank Lloyd Wright, who stays with the human scale—both plan fundamentally for the automobile. Wright's Broadacres, we shall see, is no more a city than the Ville Radieuse. On the other hand, there are those who cannot forget the vision of Sitte and want to revive the city. Their ideal for the vast metropolis is not a grand profile against the sky but the reconstitution of neighborhoods, of real cities in the metropolis where people go on their own feet and meet face to face in a square.

Housing

With the city squares of Sitte and the conception of neighborhoods as sub-cities, we return full circle from the suburban flight. Seduced by the monumental capitals of Europe, Sitte himself loses his vision and begins to talk about ornamental plazas at the ends of driveways; but the natural development of his thought would be community centers of unified neighborhoods within the urban mass, squares on which open industry, residence, politics, and humanities. (We attempt such an idea in Scheme II below, p. 162.)

Point of view: in the piazza, on the highway, from the air

An existing tendency in this direction is the community block, planned first as a super-block protected from arterial traffic, as in the *Cité Jardin*, but soon assuming also neighborly and community functions, analogous to the neighborly cooperation described by Unwin as the essence of the Garden City. Sometimes this development has led in America (as famously in Vienna) to a political banding together of the block residents, making them a thorn in the side of the authorities.

The community-block is now standard practice for all modern urban planners in all countries; but unfortunately, in this planning the emphasis is entirely on housing, and there are experts in applied sociology called "housers." "Housing" is the *reductio ad absurdum* of isolated planning. There have been cases of "housing" for workers in new factories where no provision was made for stores in which to buy food. There was a case where there was no road to the industry they worked at. Stuyvesant Town, in New York City, was built to house 8500 families without provision for a primary school. (This wretched plan, financed by a big insurance company with handsome tax relief from the city, was foisted on the city by the Commissioner against the indignant protests of a crashing majority of the city's architects. There it stands.) In better cases, the block is planned with a school and shops but not in connection with the trade or industry. The cooperative housing just now being constructed by the clothing workers' union in New York, however, is adjacent to the garment center.

The planning of housing in isolation from the total plan has, of course, been caused by scarcity, slums, war-emergency; and such reform housing has had the good side of setting minimal standards of cubic footage, density of coverage, orientation, fireproofing, plumbing, privacy, controlled rental. The bad side is that the standards are often petty bourgeois. They pretend to be sociologically or even medically scientific, but they are drawn rather closely from the American Standard of Living. The available money is always spent on central heating, elaborate plumbing, and refrigerators rather than on more space or variety of plan or balconies. And the standards are sociological abstractions without any great imaginative sympathy as to what makes a good place to live in for the people who actually live there. They are hopelessly uniform. But where is the uniformity of social valuation that is expressed in the astonishing uniformity of the plans of Housing Authorities? They are not the values of the tenants who come from substandard dwellings from which they resent being moved; they are not the values of the housers, whose homes, e.g., in Greenwich Village, are also usually technically substandard (save when they live in Larchmont). Housers do not inhabit "housing." Nor is it the case that these uniform projects are cheaper to build. The explanation is simply laziness, dullness of invention, timidity of doing something different.

To connect Housing and slum clearance is also a dubious social policy. Cleared areas might be better zoned for non-family housing or not for housing altogether; to decide, it is necessary to have a Master Plan. More important, it is disastrous to set up as a principle the concentration of distinct income-groups in great community-blocks. Suppose, for example, the entire emergency need of New York City after World War II, 500,000 units, had been met in this way; then every fifth block in the city would be marked as a tight class ghetto. To be sure such concentration presently exists, whether in slum areas or in fashionable neighborhoods; but it is worse to fix it as an official policy.

Ideally, the community block is a powerful social force. Starting from being neighbors, meeting on the street, and sharing community domestic services (laundry, nursery school), the residents become conscious of their common interests. In Scandinavia they start further along, with cooperative stores and cooperative management. Where there is a sense of neighborhood, proposals are initiated for the local good; and this can come to the immensely desirable result of a political unit intermediary between the families

The "Project"

and the faceless civic authority, a neighborhood perhaps the size of an election district. (This is what the PTA should be, and is not.) Such face-to-face agencies, exerting their influence for schools, zoning, play-streets, a sensible solution for problems of transit and traffic, would soon make an end of isolated plans for "housing."

But if the consciousness of a housing plan remains in the civic authority alone, then the super-block may achieve minimal standards and keep out through traffic, but more importantly it will serve, as we saw in the *Cité Jardin* of Le Corbusier, as a means of imposing even more strongly the undesirable values of the megalopolis.

CHAPTER 3

Industrial Plans

These are plans for the efficiency of production, treating domestic amenity and personal values as useful for that end, either technically or socially. They are first proposed for underdeveloped regions, whereas green belt planning is aimed to remedy the conditions of overcapitalization. Most simply we can think of a new industry in a virgin territory—Venezuela, Alaska—where a community can be laid out centering in a technical plant, an oilfield, a mine, or a factory, with housing and civic services for those who man the works.

Yet every use of men is also a moral plan; if it seems not to be, that itself is morally problematic. So we choose for an example the early nineteenth century New England mill town of Lowell, as a beautiful case of industrial community planning under ideal conditions in the first flush of capitalism, self-conscious as a moral enterprise. And it is the more interesting because it tries to avoid the very abuses of English capitalism that led to Garden Cities.

Another kind of underdevopment that leads to emphasis on production belongs to old but industrially backward countries that want to overtake the advanced, either to vie with them as world powers or to avoid colonial exploitation. Such was Russia, such are India and China. In these cases the emphasis is likely to be on heavy industry and the production of machine-tools, rather than on manufacture of goods for a market or the extraction of raw material for export. The product is poured back into the industry and the machinery, maintaining consumption goods and amenities near the lowest bearable point. Such a program cannot help but produce grave political and moral problems, especially among those (for instance the peasants with their traditional ways) who do not immediately appreciate the results for which they are obliged to make sacrifices. Therefore, very striking features of the program will have political rather than merely technical purposes. We have chosen to discuss here three plans of the U.S.S.R. because of the dramatic and classical conflict of the technological and political factors in Russia from 1925 to 1935. The recent spectacular effort of China follows in logical order.

But the moral-technical motivation for a kind of industrial planning springs up in a different context altogether, precisely in the most advanced and overdeveloped technologies with a vast economic and technological surplus. This is technocracy. It is the cultural emergence of engineers' values against traditional humanist or business values, as so ably championed by Veblen. In contrast to the achievements of science and engineering, the ordinary standards, expressed in the system of consumption and especially of amenity, seem irrational, a mere cultural lag. Then it is felt that by social devotion to efficiency we can liquidate the cultural lag. But the only thing that can be efficiently planned is production and the physical parts of life most like machine products. This emphasis on efficiency is apart from profit, which is seen to be systematically inefficient, and also apart from reinvestment, for there is no need for more capital; nor is it to increase the supply of goods and raise the standard of living, but to change the standard of living. The primary cultural satisfaction becomes invention; and the social virtues are, even more than efficiency, inventiveness and adaptability. Society is in process, it looks ever to the future. Ideally, there is a permanent transition.

But most people would say that the final use of any invention is consumption; to them the ideals of a technological planner like Buckminster Fuller (Dymaxion) seem even comically spiritual and austere. Yet this is a social, not necessarily a moral, contradiction of Veblen's theory, when once there is a surplus: efficient technology generates more goods and leisure and, at the same time, discourages the attitudes of consumption and waste. Some people then begin to take satisfaction in the organization of production itself; but others, we see, when they feel that nothing is *necessary* to be done, begin to kill time and decline to do anything.

A Capitalist Mill Town

The idea of a paternalistic company town, an industry and its entrepreneur providing the housing and community of its workers, goes back at least to Robert Owen's New Lanark (c. 1800), and is as contemporary as Olivetti's Ivrea in Italy. Owen's aim was to remedy a sick society and restore morale, and he looked forward, as Olivetti also seems

Part of Lowell, Mass., circa 1852 (after J. Coolidge)

to, to a kind of cooperative socialism. The expanding capitalism and individualism of the nineteenth century exploded Owen's rectangles; the Owenite communist experiment at New Harmony lasted only three years (1825–1828). But it is against this background of idealism that we must understand Francis Cabot Lowell's capitalist project for a textile town that eventuated, after his death, in the town of Lowell, Massachusetts (1823). Power-spinning had been introduced in the previous decades, and in 1814 Lowell had set up the first successful power-loom in Waltham. It was the industry of these machines, protected by the first tariff in 1816, that supported the immensely profitable new community on the Merrimack River.

The story of the founding, the two successful decades, and the decline of the ideal community at Lowell is told in J. P. Coolidge's *Mill and Mansion*. This book is beyond praise as a social study, a critique of achitecture, and analysis of community planning, so that it is here our grateful task simply to summarize some of its contents.

Francis Lowell's plan was as follows: to find a river with a rapids and dig a canal leading around it; on this island to build the mills of the associated entrepreneurs, and across the canal the housing for the several classes of operatives and management; then a main road, with shops, public buildings, and parks; and beyond the road, unplanned land for the bourgeoisie investors, traders, non-industrial townspeople. Lowell, Massachusetts, is in fact zoned in this way (though the symmetry had to be sacrificed to the topography).

The housing proved to require five classes, distinct in location and style, and from these we can at once read off the social plan:

1. Corporation executives: a tight little oligarchy in their private mansions.
2. Skilled workers: junior executives, foremen, English craftsmen to do the printing of the textiles. Housing for families in row tenements.

3. Unskilled operatives of the mill: these are the heart of the scheme; they are farm girls from the surrounding regions, housed in small dormitories in large boarding houses under strict moral and religious supervision. (As a French observer said, "Lowell resembles a Spanish town with its convents, but in Lowell you meet no rags or Madonnas, and the nuns of Lowell, instead of working sacred hearts, spin and weave cotton.")

4. Day-laborers, mainly Irish, to dig the canals and lay the bricks. Housed in makeshift huts.

5. Across the road, hotels and miscellaneous dwellings for the watchful investors, commercial travelers, lawyers, ministers, speculators, and shopkeepers.

This was in the heyday of expanding capitalism. The paternalism resided in an impersonal corporation and the laws of the market, not in a man like Owen; yet the investors were *not* rentiers, for they were watchful and sometimes intervened. Nor were the young women operatives merely a proletariat, trapped from the cradle to the grave, for they had independent purposes: they were saving for marriage, supporting parents, keeping a brother or fiancé in school; savings accounts were considerable; most of the women remained only three or four years, yet there were always replacements, for the conditions were satisfactory. Work was sunrise to sunset, but the food and social environment were good. (In his *American Notes* the astonished Dickens saw that the girls had joint-stock pianos in their boarding houses, and that they put out a literary magazine! They also wore attractive clothes.) Also, this manufacture was in the total framework of an expanding capitalist technology and economy: one of the first railroads in the county was run to Lowell and the legislators in Washington, had laid a protective tariff against European cloth. Many new processes and machines were first invented at these New England mills. Some, e.g., Amoskeag, made their own bricks (and still in New England those red or orange factories stand there, severe but not unlovely).

It was the theory of Adam Smith: many individual wills, great and small, freely cooperating in a vast plan, because it is the nature of economic man. (It is just such a situation that Prince Kropotkin shrewdly points to as an argument for anarchism—the example he uses is the railroad-network of Europe laid down and run to perfection with no plan imposed from above.)

In reading about Lowell, one is profoundly struck by the importance of ideological pressure to keep people moving in the plan, not otherwise than now in China. Strict morality and religion kept things on schedule. The girls were scrupulously honest, no need to check up on their accounts. Sexuality was taboo, family life at a distance—back on the farm or in Ireland—a goal to work for. The girls were literary, were lectured by Ralph Waldo Emerson, and wrote inspirational or romantic nature poetry; but theater was discouraged, architecture plain indeed, and we can be sure those pianos played few dance tunes. Indeed, the ideology sometimes wins out over the economy, as when the Corporation vetoed the expense for schools, but the church won out and built them. The democratic and puritanic mass agitated for Temperance, Anti-Slavery, and even, though the companies forbid, the Ten-Hour Day. There was rudimentary organization of labor and, in 1836, a strike. The architecture too everywhere proved the integration of the ideological and industrial plan: buildings were "functional" in the sense that they were what people of the time considered "appropriate" (we are reminded of Sullivan's "a church must look like a church"); we must not then hope for new style or beauty, but the excellence consists in the communal integrity.

So Lowell existed for twenty years as planned. (Dickens visited in 1842.) But it is not necessary to ask critical questions about this utopian capitalist plan, for history asked and answered the questions. When steam power became readily available because the railroads could haul coal, the water-mills had to compete. They then cut wages and the fringe benefits that made Lowell plausible as a community.

They could not compete, there was unemployment; and add the business cycle endemic in the system. Boarding houses ceased to get their subventions, the standard of living fell. Corporation land was speculated away and the zoning was broken. Meantime, as conditions deteriorated and the growing town offered other possibilities, the skilled workers, restive at the restrictions, moved away on their own. The huts of the Irish and the French-Canadians degenerated into slums. New England farmers were going west; the girls began to be foreign-born, and the boarding house system, that had been cheerful and harmonious when the girls came from like background and culture, now became untenable. Top management itself, which in the first generation consisted of entrepreneurs, succumbed to nepotism and petty tyranny. These causes exacerbated one another, and, in brief, the New England capitalist idealism that had started with the resolve *not* to repeat the conditions of the English factory-system, succumbed to the chaos of mature nineteenth-century capitalism. Lowell became a third-rate company town.

Moscow, 1935

Let us leap forward a century, and to a country where the old capitalism had never matured, but a kind of socialist system was struggling to find its forms.

The debates prior to the Russian Second Five-Year Plan brought forth four important community proposals, accepted or rejected:

1. The political-industrial concentration at Moscow;
2. The "left deviation" of the functionalists;
3. The plan of the Disurbanists;
4. The "elimination of the difference between city and village."

Of these, the first three are essentially transitional industrial plans aimed at increasing productivity, and belong in

Proposal for Red Square: proletarian "modern" (1930's)

this chapter. The fourth plan is more integral; it was a community idea proposed by Marx and Engels for advanced countries, and we shall discuss it later (p. 96 ff.).

The planning of Moscow became a problem of the Russian economic program after the first Five-Year Plan. By this time a major change had occurred in the city. In 1914 it had been a place of predominantly light industry (75%); by 1932 it had become a place of heavy industry (53%). These industries, metallurgy and electricity, were increasingly concentrated and vast. Population had increased by 73% and the total industry by 200%. Yet community services had increased only 50%. (In America, too, of course, "public services" have fallen far behind the expanding economy; but the increase of "services" in general has outstripped the increase in production and consumption goods.)

This development naturally caused an outcry on the part of consumers and residents. This was the so-called "right deviation" and was soon stifled, for "otherwise," in the words of Kaganovich, the commissar of transport, "it would be useless to hope for the consolidation of the dictatorship of the proletariat and the up-building of socialism." Equating, that is, the emphasis on heavy industry, the upbuilding of socialism, and the First Five-Year Plan.

With the Second Plan, however, the country was "entering into socialism," and this was the time to plan, on the basis of heavy industry, for communities of work and residence. The "left deviation," we shall see, denied that the first period had yet passed, and planned accordingly. In general, the right held that socialism was established in 1917–22, the center in 1927–32, the left that it was not yet begun. The factual political question, as to who is right and what kind of socialism is implied, is, fortunately, beyond the scope of this book.

We may compare the plan for Moscow with the New York Regional Plan of nearly the same time. Both develop an existing concentration of industry and residence, attempt to relieve congestion, and to limit future expansion: Moscow from 3½ to 5 million, the New York metropolitan area from 12 to 21 million. But the differences are salient. One is struck by the initial willingness of the Russians to debate quite fundamental changes, and their decision to make a city of a definite kind; whereas New York still does not have a Master Plan, though it has a Planning Commission. Moscow was to be a place of heavy industry and proletarian politics and culture, a symbolic capital of the Union. This political industrial amalgam is the key to understanding the plan.

The following main proposals were rejected: To extend the Moscow area enormously, to surround the center with a green belt and construct residential satellites (plan devised by May). This was called, in their rhetoric, a rightist counter-revolutionary attempt to weaken the city by separating the proletariat from the technology both physically and ideologically. Its affiliation with the rightism of light industry and consumption goods is plain, for it is really a Garden City plan aimed at amenity.

On the other hand, they rejected the contention of disurbanists and functionalists that all large cities were a bourgeois hangover, not socialist but state-capitalist; that the period of transition to socialism required, not improving old Moscow, but every sacrifice for industrial efficiency, even ribbon-development and residential barracks; and that the future socialist culture belonged ultimately to community blocks and their communes, without metropolitan features. (We shall consider these points on their merits in the next section.) These arguments were branded as subtly counter-revolutionary: either petty bourgeois or an attempt to damage the morale of worker and peasant. Large cities were, it was said, technologically necessary for the "concentration of capital," and, to quote a curious enthymeme of Kaganovich, "Since Moscow and Leningrad played a major part in the revolution and have won the adherence of the peasant masses, any effort to reduce the large cities is nonsense not worth serious attention."

This last argument is political, but the apparently economic argument about the concentration of capital is also really political, for the technological accumulation of capital rarely requires concentration in one area. The meaning is rather what Marx calls the "centralization of capital" in a few hands for ownership and control (*Capital*, i, xxv).

Still another rejected proposal was the Ville Radieuse of Le Corbusier: to leave old Moscow as a museum city and build on a new site. This was (mildly) called unhistorical; it disrupted community feeling, and was anyway utopian, beyond their means. A more moderate proposal, to relocate the existent scattered factories, was also called impossible, though under stress of the war far greater changes were soon made.

Instead of all these we have a plan for Moscow (1) As a capital of the dictatorship of the proletariat as a regime of heavy industry passing ideally, not yet actually, into socialism; and (2) To be a·political and cultural symbol for the nation, especially the peasants. Let us see what this means in various aspects.

The subway. With the enormous expansion of population and industry, there was a fabulous shortage of transportation and housing. The radical remedy proposed for transit was the subway, though this was opposed by both leftists and disurbanists as "an anti-social form of transportation." But the government made of its construction a remarkable labor of social devotion and solidarity; masses took part in the unskilled labor; the stations were elaborately decorated as a source of social pride; and the finished product became a byword among the peasants who cherished the opinion that it was the only subway in the world. To be sure it cannot solve the transit problem; the population limit of 5 million does not hold; there will be flight from the center and perhaps blight, as everywhere else. The technically workable solution would be to break up the industrial concentration and to separate at least the political and industrial concentrations; but these were just what was to be avoided.

Palace and Housing. Instead of at once pouring all available nonindustrial energy into the relief of the housing shortage (4½ sq. meters per person in 1935), the plan marked immense sums for enlarging and ennobling the government buildings, climaxing in the Palace of the Soviets, the most ambitious political structure in the world. (Luckily for the history of esthetics, this expression of the withering away of the State has not eventuated.) And even the future housing envisaged for the end of the ten-year period was below American minimum standards, but identical with British standards. The kind of housing is urban-industrial, large apartment houses. The country beyond the green belt is for vacationists.

The method of building is neither the mass-production proposed for the Ville Radieuse, nor yet the meticulous trade-union building of the Garden City; but it is the rationalized labor of Stakhanovism, drawing on the social enthusiasm and personal concern of each worker competing, the combination of transitional technology with symbolic socialism.

Co-operatives and Democratic Centralism. In the residential districts, existent and proposed, it was decided to disband the larger unities of 15 to 20 apartment houses, on the

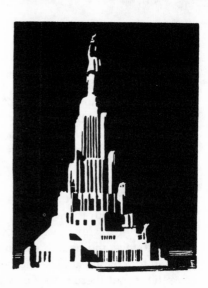

*Proposed Palace
of the Soviets (1930's)*

grounds that they were inefficient and bureaucratic. Instead, each house, managed by its tenants, is responsible to the city administration, the Moscow Soviet, through a system of sectional units, determined from above, with which to lodge complaints and suggestions. This is the end of the relatively autonomous community-block of which we spoke above. Correspondingly, the important social services of restaurants and schools would be developed by Mossoviet, though the nurseries remain, apparently, under the unit houses. That is, in general responsible control comes from above, but facility for discussion is provided below. This is the policy of the Democratic Centralism of the dictatorship of the proletariat.

Consider a case. It is hardly likely that the free, organized consumer, the autonomous community-block, would unanimously propose the construction of the Palace (or the subway) in lieu of new housing; yet with the patriotism sprung from the fact that it is his own socialism he is building, a man might readily approve the plan handed down. This is the neat—and awkward—adjustment on which the Moscow plan is based.

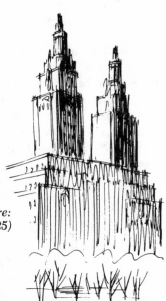

"Capitalist" architecture:
N. Y. (1925)

University of Moscow
(circa 1939)

Small industry and local control. On the other hand, a valid distinction of wide applicability now first appeared in the plan: heavy industry is controlled by the central commissariats; but small industries, especially of consumption goods and local town services (except for Moscow) are bidden to operate on their own initiative through local soviets. "The Supreme Council of National Economy cannot occupy itself with door-catches."

Obviously, during the technical transition, the small industries would find it hard to get labor and material; by 1935 local industry accounted for only 10% of the total production (J. Jewkes). But conceive this principle operating in an advanced surplus technology. Then, precisely those goods and amenities which are most subject to personal choice would be freed from the vast economy of production and distribution—they could be locally styled and even hand-made; whereas the production goods, which are more like means and less like ends, could be nationally planned and machine-analyzed.

Esthetics. The analysis we have been advancing explains the style of the Palace and the general cultural tone of the second Five-Year Plan. It is a political rather than an integrated social esthetics. The style is half baroque dreams remembered from czarism and half imitations of American capitalist cities. It is an attempt to evoke social solidarity through pride and grandeur; while the fundamental industrialization is expressed only by showing workers in overalls, it has no esthetic expression. Yet many of the designs are as ugly as can be, and it is hard to believe that they are the only possible popular appeal—*no* taste is that vulgarized. (To give a fair analogy: it is hard to believe that our TV programs are the only possible popular ones—for nobody is that idiotic.)

During the '20's, the U.S.S.R. had welcomed the vanguard of art, for instance the International Style in architecture (imported often without a just analysis of different technical resources, so that materials and construction were specified which the Russians could not provide, and fine plans made bad buildings). In cinema, Russia led the world. Then came a calamitous regression, in architecture, in cinema, in literature, in music. And the same in every social field. The sexual revolution came to an ignominious end. Progressive education was dropped. There followed (certainly partly in anticipation of the war) a solidifying of forces around national symbols, the reëmergence of ancient patriotic themes and reactionary sentiments.

Since the war, the Russian art that we have experienced —the musicians, the theater, the dancing, the painting—has been academic enough to chill your bones. It is puzzling how so much skill can be so abused.

Disurbanists and Functionalists

The scheme of the disurbanists, rejected in the Moscow debates, is an excellent adaptation of Garden City planning to the situation of a technological transition for increased productivity. "The urban concentration," they said, "is state-capitalist," and they proposed instead a lineal city laid out

Diagram of Soviet lineal city: 5-6 km. long by 2-3 km. wide; 50,000 inhabitants

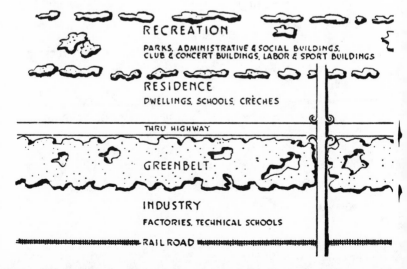

RECREATION

PARKS, ADMINISTRATIVE & SOCIAL BUILDINGS,
CLUB & CONCERT BUILDINGS, LABOR & SPORT BUILDINGS

RESIDENCE

DWELLINGS, SCHOOLS, CRÈCHES

THRU HIGHWAY

GREENBELT

INDUSTRY

FACTORIES, TECHNICAL SCHOOLS

RAILROAD

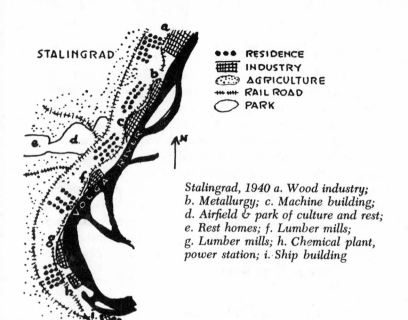

STALINGRAD

- ●●● RESIDENCE
- ▦ INDUSTRY
- ◌ AGRICULTURE
- ┿┿ RAIL ROAD
- ◯ PARK

Stalingrad, 1940 a. Wood industry;
b. Metallurgy; c. Machine building;
d. Airfield & park of culture and rest;
e. Rest homes; f. Lumber mills;
g. Lumber mills; h. Chemical plant,
power station; i. Ship building

along the routes of transportation of heavy industry. Industry and residence spread in strips along highways, railroads, and rivers, in immediate contact with the countryside. A green belt separates industry and residence. There is then an enormous economy in services, such as roads or local transit; and also an interpenetration of the rural and industrial. What is sacrificed of the classical Garden City, of course, is the attempt to make a unified center of culture and residence.

This plan was rejected as petty bourgeois: that is, it was taken as an offshoot of the separatist suburban tendency. In some ways, however, it seems to be the plan of Stalingrad (1940).

The "leftist" functionalists, on the other hand, emphasized the emergency of the transition period, claiming—as was indeed generally admitted and proved to be the case— that the technical emergency was the prelude to a military emergency. They accordingly planned for a military community, camp and barracks. This took the form (as devised by Sabsovich) of huge barracks for residence, each house accommodating two to three thousand, without private kitchens, laundries, or apartments. There were no family rooms and no general rooms, but every worker had a small separate room, as at a Y.M.C.A. Likewise, the public appearance of the community was strictly functional; the streets were machines for traffic; the houses turned inward away from them. (Notice that under other circumstances, these same devices would be considered amenities.) Obviously this proposal was exactly contrary to the sentimental strengthening of morale that was essential in the plan for Moscow.

Both disurbanists and functionalists advanced ideas also looking toward the socialist society, after the transition. The disurbanists argued that in socialism there would be an even spread of population throughout the country, bringing the city to the peasants. The leftists argued that in socialism the manner of residence would be in democratic centers not subordinate to the city gridiron, that is, in community-blocks.

China

Twenty years later, in the effort to industrialize China, we find that it is precisely the two rejected plans of disurbanists and functionalists that have become the guiding prin-

Calligraphs (reading from left): Small—tackle only things within your ability. Earth—native land, use native ingenuity. Group—community action as opposed to individual

ciples. As happened in Moscow, the Chinese Communists first built up several vast urban concentrations of heavy industry; but now it is held that the right method is (1) To industrialize without urbanizing: that is, to decentralize as much as possible, spreading small-scale modern technology among the peasants; and (2) To organize all the millions of China along military lines, with barracks-life and canteen meals, to "work as if fighting a battle, live the collective way."

The official analysis of the situation is somewhat as follows: China, unlike Russia, was hardly industrialized to begin with. She must start from scratch but therefore, also, need not repeat the urban forms that are outmoded. What China does have, however, is man power, and this, used in socially cooperative units, can transform the country in short order. (The optimum size of a commune is considered to be 5000, which happens to be also a common American optimum figure for a neighborhood.) Great reliance is placed on social enthusiasm—the Chinese, it is said, are governed not by men and not by laws, but by movements. They hope to wipe out illiteracy in a year and change to the commune system in five days! But even if this program were not inherently desirable, it would be necessary, because there is a war-emergency, the threat of returning colonialism. The general slogan is, "A few years of hard life, a thousand years of happiness."

The scheme proposes a maximum of regimentation and absorption into the social effort, destroying family and individuality. In Shanghai, we are told, no one may have a private teakettle, he must take his tea with the others. And the odd insistence on twice-daily public calisthenics for everybody certainly sounds like the morale-building (or morale-breaking) techniques of the American armed forces. We must remember, though, that Chinese farmers, in their old "extended families" of 50 to 100, were not individualistic to start with. And it is salutary for us to think of the startling comparison between the puritanical total regulation of these communes and Lowell, Massachusetts, 1823. (The difference, of course, is that, blackballed at Lowell, one could go elsewhere; whereas ostracized from a commune one might as well commit suicide.)

Positively valuable is the store set on small enterprise in advanced technology, making do with local resources, native ingenuity. For whether or not such effort *is* more efficient in the long run (and that is by no means decided), there is no doubt that it is more humanly satisfactory. The pathos is that the "advanced technology" is probably already pretty outmoded.

Here again, as in the previous industrial plans of this chapter, there is an astonishing emphasis on ideology through slogans, symbolic pictures, and street parades with drum and cymbals to announce a new high in production. "We must conquer the Gobi desert, and be first of the oil wells in China." "We hope that as pen-pushers we will be as effective as you with your shovels." People pledge to take no vacation till the quota is attained. They are intensely ashamed to be photographed by a Westerner in their age-old poverty, which they are sure he is doing as counter-propaganda (Cartier-Bresson). The motto of 1958, "Still bigger, still better, more quickly, more frugally," does not quite square with the ideal of small local enterprises—the social optimum of 5000 is soon abandoned for reasons of production; but consistency is not a necessary virtue of rhetoric.

Yet even apart from rhetoric, they seem to have a religious faith in education and science. Each commune must maintain a "university" (technology and Marxist classics are the subjects)—the money reserved for it may not be used to buy a needed tractor. Continuing the movement of 1919, the ancient writing, from right to left, up and down, is reformed to the Western way in order to admit chemical and mathematical formulae and the Arabic numerals. A farm cooperative will have, as well as a happy home for the aged and centers for agricultural machinery and transport, a "science research laboratory" and a laboratory for researching "the transformation of body wastes into electrical power." "The baptism of work and study will make a transformation of the country culturally, and the individual's transformation through work." The perfect great pilot commune is named Sputnik after the man-made moon.

Dymaxions and Geodesics, 1929–1959

If we now turn to technological planning in an advanced country, like the United States, we find that it implies a radically new analysis of living standards and values. "The designer," says Buckminster Fuller, "must provide new and advanced standards of living for all people of the world . . . Implicit is man's emancipation from indebtedness to all else but intellect." It is noteworthy that for Fuller, unlike many

Marine Corps transports Geodesic dome (1950)

so-called "technocrats"—and of course unlike the planners of backward countries we have been discussing—the problem transcends national boundaries and is worldwide. Fuller also is the modern planner who lays most stress on air travel, and modern man's extraordinary mobility. The key concept of planning turns out to be logistics, how to move masses from place to place, and how to lighten the masses to be moved.

In 1929 Fuller believed his Structural Study Associates to be the appropriate organ for the new architecture. Twenty years later, with increasing public success and (one presumes) increasing loneliness, he speaks of the Comprehensive Designer, a term, like Wright's Universal Architect, that used to be attributed to the deity. "The Comprehensive Designer is preoccupied with anticipation of all men's needs by translation of the ever-latest inventory of their potentials." The designer is the "integral of the sum of the product of all specializations."

In general, Fuller's plans amalgamate technical, ethical, and metaphysical principles. Thus, mass production is the new phase of Christianity where all men are again brothers. The obstacle to happiness is the clinging to material, especially landed, property; progress consists in "ephemeralization," dematerializing, and impermanence or process of experience and control. The handling of steel in tension, or of geodesic struts, is our progress from the "darkness of complete and awful weight to eternal light which has no weight." Architectural service is a corporate and anonymous devotion to scientific analysis "after the manner of the Ford planning department"; or it is logistical analysis that could be run on a computer, presumably like the Rand Corporation.

But the fundamental element of the plan, the invention on which Fuller rests, is the individual isolated shelter, the Dymaxion house. Fuller believes that it was only to diminish drudgery by mass services that men congested in cities, but such conveniences can be better built into a mass-produced

house as into an automobile. Mankind will then disperse.
The house must be lightweight and without foundations, to
be picked up (in 1930 by dirigibles) and dropped anywhere. Or, in the style of Le Corbusier's thinking, it makes
no difference where the man moves, since the dwellings are
machines indifferently the same everywhere. The Dymaxion
house is "free as a ship of public utilities, sewerage, water,
and other systems of the political hangnail variety." It
achieves its independence, for instance from electric power,
partly by means of machines that have not yet been invented.

The house is suspended from a central mast, using the
superior tensile strength of steel; it is hexagonal, so its members can be triangulated. Its weight per cubic foot is one-
fifth that of the ordinary dwelling. It can be assembled from
its parts in 24 hours, as well as carried through the air en
bloc. It is designed for a specific longevity and is then to be
turned in for an improved model. It thus involves the minimum of commitment to site and tradition. It is a machine
for realizing what Fuller calls the "Eternal Now." But although it is a machine, it seems to be conceived on the model

First Dymaxion house (1929), proposed as a "minimum"

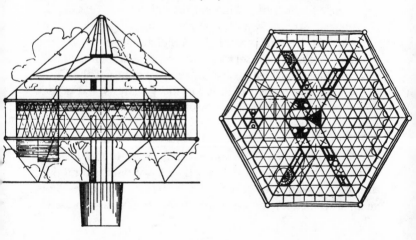

Geodesic dome at Trade Fair, Afghanistan (1956)

of a man, for its organic machinery—sun-machine, Diesel engine, septic tank, etc.—is contained in the central mast, since happy life is planned from inside out. (The "geodesic dome"—a shelter based on a system of tetrahedrons—can be used for "a theater, civic center, bank, tank-car repair area.")

Conversely, the mechanics of the human body are analyzed into automotive functions, "nerve shock-proofing," "fueling," "muscular nerve and cellular realignment" (equals sleeping), "refusing" (equals elimination). With this analysis Fuller persistently attacks the kind of psychoanalysis that gives to the organic functions a rather different importance.

A "town plan"—e.g., for Grand Rapids, Mich. (1956)— is a "geodesic environment control," and is grounded in the proposition that "man's minor ecological pattern" (meaning the immediate space he lives and moves in, as a tree in the ground) "must now be made to serve his major ecological patterning" (in an air-borne worldwide technology). "This ecological concept abandons customary classification of man's housing functions as 'urban,' 'suburban,' 'farm,' 'vacation resort,' or 'camp.'" So a typical town plan of Fuller shows the land mass of the earth distributed around the North Pole. Location is determined by the great circles, the prevalent winds for transport and the isotherms of the temperate zone for residence. Only the temperate zone, believes Fuller, produces free civilization; subtropical peoples are doomed to "semi-fascism." (It is remarkable how technocrats, unlearned in the humanities, gravitate to thinking of either this kind or of somatic morphology.) Topographical features, like other landed property, are of little account. In general, there is "centralization of mental activity, decentralization of physical activity (personal, communal, industrial)." A kind of industrial center exists at the cross of the figure-eight of the world winds, at Chicago. The "tactical center" is on the Spanish Riviera—a lovely climate, but isn't it a little lazy?

All this was to be financed, in the thirties which had a good deal of talk of monetary reform, by "time-energy industrial credits. With automatic minimum existence credits selectively contractable . . . based on foot-pounds per hour of physical effort, with time-study credits for labor-saving contributions of individual activity . . . plus sex-segregated maintenance of antisocial laggards." This economy is "integrally germane to the successful establishment of the Shelter Reproduction Industry:" that is, a combination of the specie of the technocrats (1932) with the credit system of Social Credit. Later, Fuller adds to these a system of mass speculation in industrial securities, betting on ten-cent shares in machines at the corner drug store, if there were a corner.

Politics Fuller liquidates as a system of bullying in which by monopoly control of city services and patents, a small group has the whip hand over the rest. "Universal Architecture is the scientific antidote for war."

There is also a Dymaxion esthetics and psychology. The psychology is behaviorism, grounded in the primary aversions to noise and falling. Values are analyzed as follows: previous plastic art was bound to space and the past time of tradition; the new essence of design is time-control. The esthetic standard, mass-producible, is the group ideal, and this ideal is the progression toward "material unselfconsciousness." The aim of life is to release the "residuary mental or time-consciousness, eliminating the fallacial autosuggestive phenomena of past and future, to the infinity of delight of the Eternal Now." But isn't it pathetic how this philosopher has to do such a song and dance to reach the ideal that a Taoist or Zen Buddhist aims at by just the opposite means, of sitting in your skin and breathing softly. Think Western!—there must be a harder way to do it.

The Christianity envisaged here is close to what Benjamin Nelson has called the "Universal Otherhood," the brothers are all equal by being equally isolated from one another and from God. There is nothing said about the ordinary communal activities of political initiative or non-scientific communication; even sex seems to have no social side. (And Fuller seems strangely unfamiliar with the actual psychology of the great innovators in science and art.) But how much of this is the climax of the solitude of commercial and industrial captains and how much is the final cowering of the little man from bullies who have disrupted his little peace, it is not necessary to inquire.

What standards of personal and social satisfaction do in fact spring from an advanced technical attitude?

The classical answer is Veblen's: a moral attitude composed of craftsmanship and the knowledge of the causes of things, without a taste for luxury consumption and gambling. Neither Fuller nor any other major planner gives this answer, which we therefore try to develop independently below (Chapter 6).

Instead, Fuller makes a sharp distinction between three groups: universal architects, common laborers, and consumers. To the first group he assigns the Veblenesque virtues: self-effacement, service, efficiency, openness to change. The mass labor of industry does not have this unifying spirit, its worth is measured in foot-pounds of effort, a curious standard in modern technology where the energy of human beings ranks far below coal, oil, waterfalls, and beasts of burden—we are suddenly back to China. The exercise of labor is rationalized by experts into "therblig" units of elementary muscular contractions.

Fuller's theory of consumption is introduced by the following telling analysis: "In the early days of the motor car it was not only a common affair but a necessary one that the owner be as familiar with the lingo of the carburetor as the manufacturer . . . Since these days, industrial progress has developed what may be termed 'consumer's delight,' progressively less technical, and less self-conscious, control of the mechanical composition produced by industry . . . There has developed an extraordinary multiplicity, of selecting and refining details, behind the scenes." This is a remarkable expression of the Hollywood paradise of ease, all doors opening by photoelectricity. *This* is the "infinity of delight of the Eternal Now," the satisfaction of life apart from work of the hands, nature of the place, clash of opinion, continuity of the self with its past or the ego with the id. Meantime, however, the "unselfconscious" (equals progressively ignorant) consumer is in fact more and more controlled by his environment. Its reason and direction is no business of his. Yet Fuller protests that the monopoly of the city water supply is a bond of slavery! It is to be feared that the politics of this unpolitical scheme is simply a wishful control of everybody else by the self-effacing Universal Architects or Comprehensive Designers. To the masses, however, is given the precisely Unveblenesque mania of gambling on the financial future of one or another set of Structural Study Associates.

The Size of Factories

We concluded the previous chapter with a critique of housing planned in isolation from the total community. Let us here say something about the other side of the medal, the isolated planning of factories by industrial engineers rather than community architects. Such planning is an outstanding example of the social waste in neglecting the principle of minimizing whatever is neither production nor consumption.

Especially during the last war, the size of plants, sheds, factory areas, and the number of workers at the plants grew steadily. With the concentration of capital uniting under

one control—not only the different producers of a commodity but also the production of allied parts, appliances,
and by-products—there went on also the physical concentration of production in vast centers. At Willow Run a single
shed covered a span of two-thirds by one-fourth of a mile.
Glenn Martin Middle River had 3 million square feet of
floor space. A layout at Simonds Saw and Steel had eight
parallel assembly lines. Often, 50,000 workers were employed.

Now, apart from land costs, it is generally assumed that
such concentration is technically efficient. It unifies the
source of power, it brings together raw materials, parts, and
assembly, it saves on servicing the buildings. But this universal and obvious assumption is probably false; it fails to
consider the chief social expense in all large-scale production, labor time.

It is almost always cheaper to transport material than
men.

If the plant is concentrated, the bulk of workers must live
away and commute. If the plant were scattered, the workers could live near their jobs, and it is the processed materials that would have to be collected for assembly from
their several places of manufacture. (We are not here
speaking of primary metallurgy and refining.) The living
men must be transported twice daily; the material and
mechanical parts at much longer intervals.

Which transport is easier to schedule? The time of life of
a piece of steel is not consumed while it waits for its truck:
a piece of steel has no feelings. Supply trucks move at a
convenient hour, but the fleet of trams and busses congest
traffic at 8–9 a.m. and at 4–5 p.m. If the men travel by auto,
there is mass parking, with one shift leaving while another
is arriving, and the factory area must be still larger to allow
for the parking space. After one gets to this area, he must
walk to the work station: it is not unusual for this round
trip to take three-quarters of an hour. During part of this
shifting, the machinery stands still.

To be sure, most of this consumption of time and nervous

energy is not paid for, and the roads and franchises that make commutation possible are part of the social inheritance. But from the point of view of social wealth, the expense must be counted in, even though it does not technically appear in the price. The worker's time is bound and useless, even though unpaid. If parts of this expense, of time and effort, were made to appear as an item on the payroll, as in the portal-to-portal demands of the mine workers, there would soon be better planning.

What is the alleged technical economy of concentration? The first great reason for large factories was steam power—to a lesser extent, water power—the need to keep the furnaces going and to use the power to its fullest extent. When manufacturing is increasingly powered by electricity, this cause no longer exists. Second, belt-line assembly is a cause of a certain amount of concentration; but this requires a large area, not a huge area. On the contrary, the overall effect of belt-line analysis should be to decrease rather than increase the average total area, for the parts are not tailored to the product as it takes shape, but are prefabricated and therefore could be made elsewhere. What is the great advantage in parallel assembly lines? Except in the unusual case of maximum production on three shifts a day, the heating and servicing of a huge single shed is less economical than an arrangement of smaller sheds.

The fact is, of course, that—especially during emergencies—the planning is far worse than anything so far indicated. Not only is the large area planned without thought of the domestic community, but the plan is regarded solely as a problem in engineering, without thought of a labor supply. The integration of the factory with society consists in locating the area on a highway (built by town funds), whether or not there are housing, schools, etc. at the other end of the highway.

Such is the situation as of this writing, wherever labor time is the chief factor in production: to plan the separation

of the factory area and the domestic community is technically inefficient, and the huge factory area is socially un-
economical. (To the extent, and wherever, factories become
automatic, the conclusion does not follow, for the chief
expense is then in the automatic machines, which do not
commute. Nor does it follow in the extractive and metallur-
gical industries, where the raw materials and the parts are
very bulky, or the site is determined by nature.)

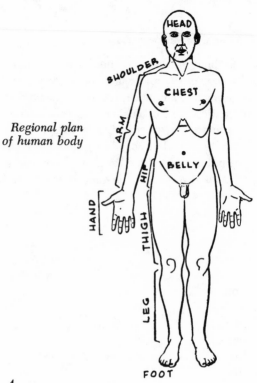

Regional plan of human body

CHAPTER 4

Integrated Plans

But let us now turn to some noble schemes that try to avoid isolated planning; they are plans for the "whole man". We saw that green belt plans were a reaction to an ugly technology and industrial plans were a reaction to poverty and colonialism; but integrated plans also are a reaction—to the loss of well-rounded humanity in modern civilized life, not otherwise than Stoics and Epicureans reacted against the follies of the city and Rousseau rebelled against the vices of the court. By and large, in the last hundred years, it is the loss of country life that bothers the planners. People begin to speak of "farming as a way of life." In Sweden, it has long been a social policy to preserve the urban-rural ratio as it was in 1800, for social stability and many-sided human development. Marx and Engels looked forward to a future, after the maximum of concentration of capital, when there would be an elimination of the difference between city and village, liquidating both "rural idiocy" and the "craft idiocy" of technicians. American regionalists often hark back to ante-bellum conditions that allowed for manners and literature.

The integration of farm and industry is also an answer to immediate scarcity and emergency. A simple example is the spinning campaign of the Indian National Congress: to ease the poverty of the peasants by the income of spinning-wheels (incidentally getting rid of the British). The Chinese, we saw, aim at heavy industrialization without urbanization. But let us quote also the following recommendations of our National Resources Planning Board, published in the depths of the depression (1934): "The integration of agricultural and industrial employment by the establishment of homes for workers employed in non-agricultural occupations, where they may produce part of their living, to become a permanent national policy; and that this policy be broadened to include: Encouraging the location of industries in rural areas now seriously deficient in sources of income . . . Encouraging the location of industries on the peripheries of large cities in definite relation to rapid transit facilities to the countryside."

In advanced technologies, one direction of integration—bringing industry to the farm—is now commonplace as co-operative or collective farming and the application of machines to diversified farming (which can indeed go to the extreme of assembly-line farming, hydroponics, incubations, etc., that could just as well be carried on in the city). The excess of this tendency, however, simply turns agriculture into another industry without the cultural values of the city, as in the vast Russian or Chinese state-farms, or in our own one-crop agriculture, whether in the great fruit plantations or in making plastics from soybeans.

The opposite direction of integration, bringing the farm

values to the city, is in advanced countries a profoundly radical proposition. The values attached to "farming as a way of life" are relative self-sufficiency, escape from the cash nexus, direct control of necessities, practical attachment to family, home, site, and natural conditions, as celebrated by Borsodi and others. Sentimentally, this tendency leads to "exurbanism," which we have discussed above as a kind of social schizophrenia. But taken seriously, it leads at once to the thorny path of founding utopian communities.

Finally, with the bringing together of the country and city we enter on regional planning, a complex in which the layout of towns, or even their existence or non-existence, is only one factor among many. It is usually agreed that every integrated plan is a regional plan. The unity of a region for integrated planning is found either in resources of land and climate and raw materials and power apt for technical development, or in concentrations of population and skills, as in the "Greater New York Regional Plan." The combination of industrial satellites and collective farms advocated by the Russians makes up a typical regional plan. And the remarkably many-sided plan of the TVA can serve us as an example of integrated primary planning unique in the United States.

Broadacres and the Homestead

The Broadacres plan of Frank Lloyd Wright could be considered as an attempt to bring farm values to an industrial town. "A human being from the time he is born," says Wright, "is entitled to a piece of ground with which he can identify himself by the use of it. If he can work on his ground, he should do it. But, barring physical disability, he should not eat if he does not work—except when he can fairly trade his right to work for some other actual contribution to the welfare and happiness of those who do work. Money is today [1937] his immunity from work, a false privilege, and because of it there is insecurity, confusion,

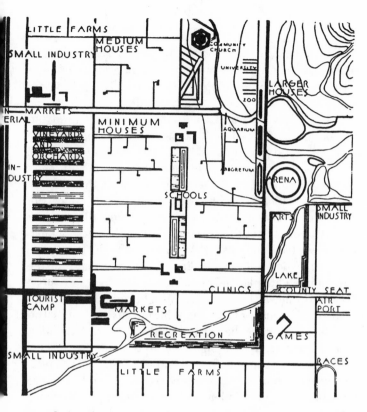

Broadacres: pattern extending over the entire countryside (after Wright)

and loss of quality in all life-values. The philosophy of every form in Broadacres is just this 'out of the ground into the light,' in circumstances that make a happy thing of man's use and improvement of *his own* ground."

This sturdy individualism is admirable; it is the archetypal attitude of the American architect, a socially respected artist who has a "profession." It does not promise much excitement, much existential novelty, nor does it do much for high culture. It sounds Jeffersonian; but Jefferson is great because of his polarity with Paris, London, New York.

The economic conception is partly from Henry George, partly from (or agreeing with) Ralph Borsodi. The value of land is given by its use; agricultural self-support is primary and the chief part of industrial culture; industrial and professional division of labor and exchange is valid but secondary; finance and most of the political superstructure are invalid and predatory. But Borsodi, planning a rural life, drives these ideas to their logical conclusion and therefore is culturally radical, whereas Wright feels that his own work is "transitional" and he is culturally tame. "We cannot yet expect everyone to become a bona-fide tiller of the soil, particularly not the citizens of such urbanized population as we have at present. We must provide for people whose education and way of life has unfitted them for the more rounded life planned here."

It is sad that, as he got older, Wright quite lost the wild vision of his youth, of flaming Chicago, its machines and blast furnaces, that he shared with Dreiser, Sandburg, *Poetry* magazine, all tending to age in the same way.

Broadacres is conceived as a kind of county seat, a relative concentration occurring occasionally in a less dense population stretching indefinitely. Even so, it provides four square miles for 1400 families, almost up to the formula "An acre per person—a maximum of, say, ten acres for a farmer." (The Garden City, we remember, has 12 families to the acre.) It is not a city plan but a continuing region, varying according to the topography. Broadacre City is "everywhere and nowhere." It stretches in all directions. For Wright the salient features of neo-technology are "automobility" and electric communication. (Does he mean TV?) Industry is decentralized to one or two moderately-sized industries in each concentration—he gives no plan of the decentralization. In general, the industrial plants are scattered among the farms. "Automobility" (car and helicopter) is the means of combining the large areas of agricultural residence with industrial work, for apparently most of the farms are maintenance gardens. That is, the formula of integration is nearer to the National Resources Planning Board's "industrial occupation plus subsistence farming" than to Borsodi's "independence farming plus cash-crops or domestic industry for the purchase of labor-saving machinery." But Broadacres is conceived not as a subsistence but as a surplus plan, it consciously selects rural values over urban values.

The politics is very confused. What belongs to the individual acre and its improvement is private; what belongs to the big machinery—e.g., roads, gasoline, power—is controlled by the democratic central government, this being the principal justification of government altogether. But "industry" as such—does he distinguish manufacture from other industry?—is under corporate capitalism, which apparently will relinquish its specific ownership of oil and power "without revolution." There are, then, one-car houses and five-car houses. Yet to avoid the dilemmas of capitalist finance, the society has Social Credit—but this, of course, would be meaningful only in an expanding profit technology, the very opposite of the Borsodian restricted non-cash economy which also seems essential to Broadacres. (What Wright could mean, and might have said if he ever thought it through, is the strictly divided economy of maintenance and surplus that we propose in Scheme III below, Chapter 7.)

"It follows from all this genuinely constructive way of life that in the administration the county architect is important. He has a certain disciplinary as well as cultural relationship to the whole, and since he maintains the harmony of the whole his must be one of the best minds the city has, and it will inevitably become the best trained." This speaks for itself.

The education of the young is agricultural. "Each boy and girl has to begin with a hoe in his hand. We begin at the root of society with the culture of the children . . . A 'classical' education would be worse than useless. Instead, man studies man in relation to his birthright, the ground. He starts his earthly career with his feet on the ground, but

his head may be in the clouds at times." Lastly (1945):
"Conscription is the ultimate form of rent."

With this architect, of course, the chief value of Broadacres would not be in its model plan, but in the concrete
buildings, in the adaptations that he would make to the
varieties of sites and local materials, and the analysis of
actual living arrangements. This is where the live culture
would appear. The beauty of Wright's architecture begins
in the expression of the site, especially a peculiar site, and
in finding the form in natural materials, especially local
materials. It is a domestic architecture, for he sees the problem of architecture as enclosure of space to make a unique
place, a shelter. The uniqueness of the place is given by
the plan, which is made for an individual family. The
machined materials are plainly machined and handled as
if tailor-made, no two houses alike. There is as much design
in a single Wright unit as in the thousand units of a housing
project, and it is more relevant design.

The importance of Broadacres as a community plan lies
in Wright's willingness to select values, going with or against
current trends as suits his free intuition. But his intuition is
limited. He aims at the integration of urban and rural life,
but he seems, by the time of Broadacres, to have lost what
feeling he had for the city and the factory. He does not
tell us how to make industrial life humane and worthwhile;

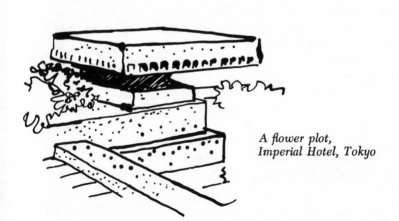

A flower plot,
Imperial Hotel, Tokyo

his presentation of industries, factories, industrial location, transport, the division of labor, is extremely sketchy, often inferior to existent facts. Yet, embarrassed to make a clean break with the city, he missed the opportunity to plan a genuinely Borsodian community, an enterprise for which he was more fitted than any other man.

The Homestead

Borsodi himself plans for only rural America: his is a plan for relative agricultural self-sufficiency and machine domestic production. He says little about cities and big industry except to advocate an even distribution of the population—50%–50% instead of 80%–20%. The reduction in industrial crops would itself have this effect. Yet much of what he says about domestic production with small electrical machines is applicable to urban life.

He has two main theses. First, as the cost of production falls, the cost of distribution rises. This is clearly true of crop production, whose industrialization involves immense areas with increasing bulk transportation, marketing, spoiling, as well as the need for cash purchases at prices which, unlike home transactions, include the wages of a host of middlemen and functionaries. (In industrial farming the land is also abused, as Kropotkin showed sixty years ago in *Fields, Factories, Workshops.*) Borsodi concluded that at least "two-thirds of the goods and services" required in a home are more efficiently produced domestically with the aid of electricity. That is, in a farm home where there is raw material.

His second thesis is that social security and stability require a larger number of self-sufficient farmers, whereas industrial cash farming has made the farmer even more insecure than his urban brother. There is an irreducible difference between diversified farming and all other work: the farmer can ultimately subsist, even in some comfort, without the industrial division of labor, but without the farmer the

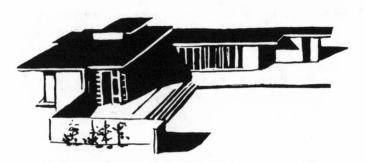

Broadacres: one-car house

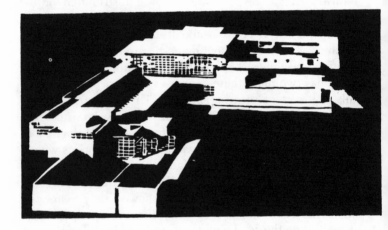

Broadacres: five-car house

non-farmer cannot subsist at all. In principle this unrecip-
rocal relation should involve a different overall social plan
from that in which farming, regarded practically as an
extractive industry, is like other businesses, only more
risky. (In philosophical economic terms the unreciprocity
could be stated by saying that the capital of a diversified
symbiotic farm is largely natural—it was not social labor

that produced the physiology, the reproductive system, and the balance of nature of plant, animal, and man. Therefore one must not look to the same extent for the relations of contract, wages, and prices.)

The farm has often provided an excellent all-around integration of work and culture. (Marx somewhere speaks of the Elizabethan yeomanry as having had the highest humanity yet reached!) Yet it is equally true that, historically, farm life and domestic life have never provided the grand breadth of political and social culture that pertains to cities. It is not only by external pressure that people have emigrated from the land when they could. The planner of integration must take the city into account and find the human scale there.

Perhaps this is a good place to mention, finally, the fact that used to haunt every discussion of country-city relations; "the primary consideration," says Lewis Mumford, "dominating every other in city-planning." Namely, that the birth rate in the country more than reproduces the population, whereas the cities must be replenished by mass migration of youth from the farm. And since taxes and so forth are determined by city politicians, the farmers get the dirty end of the stick.

In the last two war decades, however, marriage and family life have so increased in general and the farm population has so decreased, that the relationship is less clear; the suburbs seem to be the favored breeding grounds.

The Soviet Regional Plan

In a country predominantly rural, like the Soviet Union—three rural to one urban as against one to four in the United States—the problem is the reverse: political and cultural perfection is thought to depend on the diffusion of industrial labor and industrial values. The scheme of integration is not to reassert rural self-sufficiency but to bring the cities to the land. The "elimination of the difference between the

PROPOSAL 1
two cities of 150,000-
200,000 population in
favorable sites. But workers
must travel up to 22 miles
to the oil fields.

PROPOSAL 2
12 to 15 settlements
of 15,000-20,000
population—near the oil
fields. But some sites
are unfavorable and because
towns are small, municipal
and cultural services
would be limited.

PROPOSAL 3
Five cities each with
population of 60,000-
80,000, all located
favorably. Each large
enough for good culture
and municipal service. All
convenient to oil fields.

ACCEPTED—

BUT

shortage of materials retarded construction—the
increasing population crowded into Baku where
housing, schools and utilities were available
though overloaded.

CENSUS—BAKU as proposed 1942

Equals 700,000 people

actual condition 1939—809,000

$\bigwedge$ = Oil field   ■ = Inhabited place

city and the village" has two aspects: the regional decentralization of industry and the industrialization of agriculture.

At the time of the preparation of the Moscow plan, we
saw, it was counterproposed, in the interests of transportation, to decentralize heavy industry to the sources of raw
materials and power and thus to develop new, smaller centers in hitherto undeveloped regions, especially the Urals,
Siberia and the water basins in the South. This counterpro-
posal was later modified and extended into a full-blown regional plan, the "entry into socialism," the principle being
cultural as well as technical (not to mention the military
necessity of decentralizing heavy industry away from the
then German frontier).

Ideally, the industrial plan consists of an even distribution
of centers throughout the country, each with several one-
industry Satellite Towns. The even spread brings the cities to
the land, an aim so important that it can in particular cases
outweigh strict technical efficiency: e.g., the Magnitogorsk-
Kuznetsk (Ural-Siberian) iron-coal combination was perhaps less efficient than bringing the iron westward to the
coal, but it freed the heaviest industry from dependence on
Europe, gave it a mid-Union source of steel, and built up
the vast spaces of the east. (As it turned out, coal was later
found in the Urals and iron in Siberia.) The form of Satellite
Cities allows for specialization and yet regional concentration to insure a relative regional autonomy: it keeps separate industries close to the source of their materials, it is
free of the excessive local transport of great metropoles, yet
it provides a sufficient aggregate population to support an
urban culture. A typical satellite cluster, the chemical combination around Perm, is described by Hannes Meyer.

The ideal for the industrial satellite was felt to be 200,000;
compare this with the 100,000 of Sharp's culture satellite.
But in Russia, as elsewhere, the ideal often succumbs to

Proposal vs. disposal on the Baku Peninsula

circumstances. Thus, despite a reasonable decision to develop the Baku peninsula in a group of medium cities of 80,000, development centered in the city of Baku, which by 1939 had grown to over 800,000, with an increasing problem of transport to the oil wells.

To sum up the industrial plan, the aim is "To develop industries close to the sources of raw materials and power . . . To distribute industry evenly over the entire country, so as to create nuclei of industrial and urban culture in the backward peasant regions . . . To specialize production in accordance with the natural and cultural resources of each region . . . But to provide a variety of production so that

New city of Novo-Sibirsk: 1. Civic center 2. Railroad station and factory 3. Stores 4. Theater and museum 5. Parks and schools 6. Housing 7. Warehousing

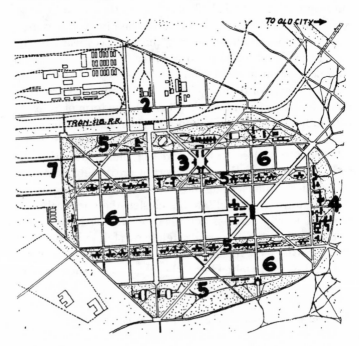

every region may achieve a relative completeness, not autarchy, within its territory." (Hans Blumenfeld.)

Politically, such a decentralized plan on the basis of industrial specialization involves two polar principles. On the one hand there must be an authoritative national plan to allot the specific production and distribute the products; and in Soviet discussion this pole is always emphasized. But we should also expect that each decentralized industrial complex, made self-conscious by its specific work and having a "certain regional completeness," would exert political power: the regional specialization of industries should produce a kind of federal syndicalism; yet this eminently interesting result has been severely unstressed by Soviet planners. On the contrary, although the revolution itself, and the very idea of soviets, sprang in great measure from industrial units acting as political powers, the tendency has always been toward political centralization.

But on the civic level, the local autonomy of towns and regions has been encouraged (somewhat like the system of states and counties in the United States). City services, housing, etc., are not determined by the national economic plan, they must be decided closer to home—provided material and capital are allotted by the central government. There is a resurgence of town soviets. But no correlation is made between town authority and the specific industrial role that gives livelihood; the great chance of integration is muffed.

The actual ideals can almost be read off from the typical town plan itself. It is, again, a green belt plan, quarantining the production from the social life; but—this is the novelty—in the center of the residential part, well removed from the factories, is the square of the national and local administration, connected by a broad avenue with the center of culture, the theater, the museum. If only it were the union-hall! As in some of our own country towns, on the square there is the church and the Grange, as well as the post office (and the jail).

The main avenues frequently follow the lineal plan of

the disurbanists, along railroad or waterway, for efficiency
of transport. But there is always the attempt to create a
political and cultural center, and to introduce the amenities
of Garden Cities. Residential quarters are community
blocks, for that is the working unit of domestic life; but the
principle of finding the working unit is not applied to the
integration of industry, politics, culture.

Thus, on the whole we see the signs of nineteenth-century
reform, but not a radical new way of life. There will be
shorter working hours, social services, and "parks of culture
and rest"; but initiative and administration, the grounds
of individual security and the culture of society, are related
only indirectly to the work and the potential power of the
people.

The Industrialization of Agriculture

The other side of the elimination of the difference between the city and the village is the industrialization of
agriculture. Because of circumstances, this has taken two
main forms, state farm and collective farm, the second
superseding the first about 1932.

In the state farm, agriculture is considered as an extractive industry on a par with other industries. Industrialization
consists in employing heavy machinery, maximum specialization of crop, and the indefinite increase in the size of the
field devoted to each speciality. The theory is that productivity is increased not only in absolute volume but economically with the increase of area devoted to a single crop.
(With Borsodi, or Kropotkin, we have seen reason to doubt
this.) The agricultural plan then proceeds as follows. First,
a national program of crop requirements and the machinery
available. Next, division of the country as a whole, mainly
according to climate, into vast zones for specialized farming:
wheat, stock, fruit, citrus fruit, cotton. The zones for perishable vegetables are, perforce, laid around the cities—but
with new methods of preservation and transport, this would
be obviated, as in America. Third, training in central agri-

cultural colleges of expert agronomists to be sent through-out the country as directors of the peasantry, who now become an unskilled proletariat.

If a crop useful in manufacture, such as cotton or soy-bean, is combined with a regional industrial center, we have a model agrindustrial complex.

On a typical state farm, 100,000 hectares, there will be a center of administration, containing shops for major ma-chine repairs and apartment houses for the winter residence of the total farm population. Such a center might well be in the city itself. The farm is divided into working sections where the machinery for each is kept during the summer, and where minor repairs are made on the spot by a traveling shop summoned from the big administrative center by telephone. The workers of each section remain in the field through the summer, in summer cottages. The harvested crop is taken by rail directly from stations in the fields. The combination of crops is not the diversification of small-scale intensive farming, but depends on the functional industrial juxtaposition of different vast farms, e.g., providing feeding stations for cattle on a neighboring corn farm. The single cash crop is marketed in Moscow and the workers are paid money wages. (The factor of distribution, of course, is enormously increased.)

Such a scheme is obviously the finish of agriculture as a way of life and of the farmer as a relatively self-subsistent craftsman with an important domestic economy. Corre-spondingly, the transition is easy from rural to canned urban values. The state farm is a remarkable pattern for getting the worst of both worlds. In any case it failed in Russia around 1930, because of political and especially technical difficulties. Such farms survive in Russia mainly as stations for experiment and breeding. (The increasing success of such cash-crop estates in America is due to our immense technology of transport and preservation, and because there are towns and cities for the rural proletariat to escape to; and add the ruthless exploitation of Mexican and Negro migratory labor.)

Collective Farms

Collective farming is an adaptation to industrial technology less disruptive of the traditional ways, which it indeed perfects.

Enough individually worked farm land is pooled to be
technically and economically practicable for machine cultivation. (Average 80 farms, 1930.) Each farm family maintains for its own use a private plot, house, and animals.
Throughout the countryside, machine stations are established by the state to serve the collectives. (One station to
40 collectives.) The stations provide not only machines and
repairs, but agronomic and social services. The tax for the

Kolkhoz: one M.T.S. per forty collective farms

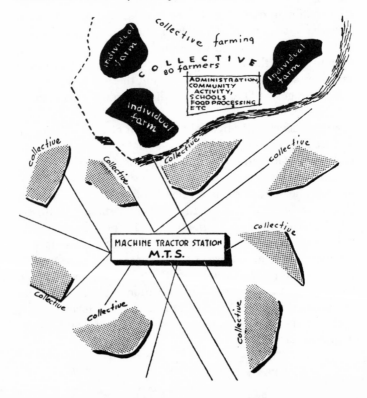

station, including insurance, comes to about 30% of the produce, paid in kind; the rest is divided among the co-operators. During the summer, a city day's work is done on the collective by the men, about half a day's work by the women; off-time can be devoted to the private holding. In addition, winter industrial work is available at processing plants located on the collectives or at the machine stations. Further, the crop produced on the collective is most often diversified; it may be sold locally, as well as consumed privately.

This seems to be a good integration. Whatever the actual practice may be, the ideal of industrialization here is not necessarily to bring the farmer into the cash nexus of the national economy, run from Moscow, but to give him in-creased productivity and easier work in his locality. The cost is a loss of individual independence, but the Russian poor peasant was never an individualist. Culturally, the scheme affirms the communalism of the peasants and allows for more rational cooperation. In a backward region, it cer-tainly means a general advance. It does not destroy the agricultural way of life, but makes the farm a more equal rival of the city.

Intentional Communities

Cooperative farming, pooling land for machine cultiva-tion, reserving part for diversified gardening, with various degrees of family ownership, all as a basis for a more inte-grated community life: this exists in many places, in cooperatives of the United States and Europe, in the impres-sive collectives of Mexico and Russia, and the communes of China. The driving motives may be economic, to get a fair deal with the city, to raise the cultural level of the peasants and rescue them from poverty, illiteracy, and dis-ease, to industrialize without urbanizing, etc. Such motives can be part of national policy.

It is a very different matter when the way of life itself,

a well-rounded life in a free community, is the principal motivation. Such an attitude belongs not to backward but precisely to avant-garde groups, who are sensitive and more thoughtful than the average, and who react against the extant condition of society as fragmented, insecure, lonely, superficial, or wicked. They are willing to sacrifice social advantages to live in a community of the like-minded. National policy and policy-makers are not up to these refinements; the communities are small, politically on the fringe (though often intensely political as a function of life), and they tend to be transitory; yet they are the vital engaged experiments in which, alone perhaps, new social ideas can emerge, so we must notice them here.

Such "intentional communities," as the sociologists call them (modern examples are described by H. Infield), have come into being throughout history—in antiquity as philosophic or mystical brotherhoods; then as Christian fellowships; during the Reformation as part of the general dissent; as ways of coping with early industrial capitalism (Owenites, Fourierists). But our modern conditions, of superorganized capital and one neo-technology after another, have perhaps added a new chapter to the old story. To put it paradoxically, there is today so much communication, means of communication, and communication-theory, that there isn't any community; so much socialism, social-agency, and sociology that there isn't any society of work and living. We have mentioned these absurdities in our introduction; they induce "utopian" reactions, for instance our harping here on "integration."

Consider our modern difference another way. Intentional communities have generally disintegrated, or so their members thought, because of outside pressures or outside temptations, bankruptcy, hostility of the surroundings, loss of religious faith among skeptics, attraction of big-city vices. It is generally agreed that non-rational motives, like religion or nationalism, wear better in this struggle than rational motives like philosophy, pacifism, or economic good sense.

But today we also think that communities disintegrate especially because of interpersonal difficulties; these explain the boredom, inefficiency, loss of faith; people are simply not up to living and working together. So the experts in community give sociometric tests (Moreno) to determine who among modern men are fit to live closely with their fellows, to bear the tensions and excitements of it. "Integration" is apparently no longer natural for all men. This seems to cut down the possibilities enormously, for to live well now requires, (1) To be disgusted with the common way; (2) To have a burning ideal to share, and (3) To have a cooperative character.

Given the paucity of candidates, such weeding-out tests are a poor expedient. Would it not be better, instead of regarding "non-cooperation" as a datum, to take the bull by the horns and regard community life as a continuous group-psychotherapy in our sick society, in which just the anxieties and tensions of living together become the positive occasions to change people and release new energy altogether? This would in turn diminish the reliance on non-rational ideals, since the excitement of contact is soon more valuable than the attractions of the world.

Kvutzah

The most perfect viable intentional community of modern times has been the kvutzah or kibbutz of the Zionists and Israelis. Those who settled these little communities were leaving not only anti-Semitism but also, imbued with the most advanced organic and socialist philosophies of the nineteenth century, the inorganic and competitive world of the west. As Jews, farming seemed to them the return to primary usefulness, independence, and dignity from which they had been excluded; but many of them were also professionals and craftsmen, used to science and machines. They had also a pioneering dedication to a neglected and inhospitable soil, with the satisfaction of making it

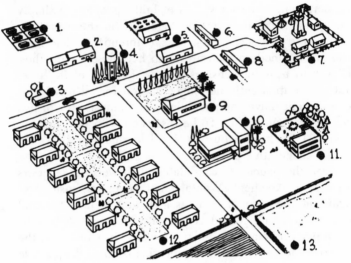

1. POULTRY RUNS
2. SHEDS
3. LAUNDRY & BATHROOMS
4. WATER TOWER
5. STABLES
6. WORKSHOPS
7. FORT
8. GARAGE
9. CULTURE
10. DINING HALL
11. CHILDREN'S HOUSE & SCHOOL
12. LIVING QUARTERS
13. FIELDS

Kibbutz

bloom. This was sharpened by nationalism, for the land was foreign and became increasingly hostile. Pretty soon they learned that this arduous community was not for everybody, and their international organization coped with the weeding-out by setting up long training periods for candidates before the emigration.

In its heyday, unlike the Russian collective, the kvutzah exercised almost complete autonomy of activity, and yet could sell in a competitive market; it was a community-anarchism that, apart from its nationalism, would have satisfied Kropotkin. Crops, methods, industrialization, education, family relations, interpersonal problems: all directly determined in town meeting. Unhampered by national planning bureaucrats, each community can make use of the skills and resources it happens to have, and manufacture shoes, bricks, processed foods, citrus products—whatever seems convenient and profitable. Also, by entering into exchange with other autonomous communities of the same kind—for they form an even international federation—they partly avoid the stranglehold of the cash nexus. There is at least the nucleus of a sufficient technology initiated and governed completely from below.

More remarkable than making the desert bloom, these communities have invented, and somewhat proved, a new idea about the upbringing of children. The parents have private quarters, which provide home, love, and emotional security also for the children; but the education and discipline of the children belongs to the entire community, peers and the productive life of the adults: more objective and friendly than parents. (This requires, of course, a small community where everybody knows everybody. When the kvutzah grows beyond this it must split up.) The young people of this training whom one meets—"cactus-fruit," as they call themselves—are, as one would expect, characteristically brash, good-looking, know-it-all but not disrespectful, self-reliant but not really independent, sentimental, and very provincial. The brand of an integrated community, better than other brands.

Naturally, with the establishment of the national state, these communities are under heavy pressure. Community anarchism does not fit easily into national states—especially when the overseas aid that has greased the wheels of the Zionist enterprise begins to dry up. Yet in the great present crisis, the unexpected influx of hundreds of thousands of refugee Jews from the surrounding Moslem countries, the communities have been willing and able to receive and train far more than their share: they are stable and adaptable. In the long run, perhaps, the more dangerous threat to their existence is the attraction of urban life.

Progressive Schools

A major problem of every intentional face-to-face community is its "cash-crop," its economic role in the great
society that has no integral way of life but has a most integrated cash nexus. Usually the problem is not enough money
or credit to buy needed mass-produced machinery. But
let us mention a touching example of a contrary problem.
The Macedonia (pacifist) community made pedagogic toy-
blocks for cash, and distributed them, at cost of production,
to like-minded groups like progressive schools; but the
blocks became popular and big commercial outfits wanted a
large number. Macedonia was then faced with the following
dilemma: these commercial jobbers would resell at a vast
profit; yet if Macedonia itself charged them what the market
would bear, the community would itself be contaminated
by commercialism.

The cash-crop of the small intentional community that
has often served as its social role in the larger society is
education: the community is a progressive school. (One is
reminded of Plato's remark that training men is like tending
livestock, so that this too is a branch of agriculture.) In the
theory of progressive education, integral community life is
of the essence: one learns by doing, one learns to live in a
contactful community. The buildings are built by the students and teachers. Usually there is a farm. Emphasis is laid
on creative arts and crafts, as unblocking of deep energy and
as inventing the forms of better environment. Some progressive schools specialize in serving the surrounding region
as social-physicians and leaders of regional improvements.

In the educational community, the mores are in principle
permissive and experimental, and the persons form, almost
invariably, a spectrum of radical thought and life, from
highly moralistic religious-pacifists, through socialists and
La Follette or TVA liberals, to free-thinking anarchists. The
close contact of such persons, the democratic and convivial

intermingling of faculty and students, leads inevitably to violent dissensions, sexual rivalries, threatened families. It is at this point, as we have said, that the community could become a psychotherapeutic group and try by its travails to hammer out a new ideal for us all in these difficult areas where obviously our modern society is in transition. Instead, the community itself tends to break up.

Yet perhaps the very transitoriness of such intensely motivated intentional communities is part of their perfection. Disintegrating, they irradiate society with people who have been profoundly touched by the excitement of community life, who do not forget the advantages but try to realize them in new ways. People trained at defunct Black Mountain, North Carolina, now make a remarkable little village of craftsmen in Haverstraw, N. Y. (that houses some famous names in contemporary art). Perhaps these communities are like those "little magazines" and "little theaters" that do not outlive their first few performances, yet from them comes all the vitality of the next generation of everybody's literature.

Regionalism

Let us, finally, say something about regionalism and regional-planning. Nearly all American planners would agree that these are grand things, reacting, no doubt, not only against isolated planning but against the sameness sinking down on our country from coast to coast. But as Charles Abrams said recently (Tokyo, 1958), it is hard to say what they mean by regionalism, what is the unifying principle of a region. (He himself tends to find it either in administrative convenience or in some primary geophysical development, like planning a watershed.)

The Russian regional plans of this chapter are industrial-economic unities, and these regions may well, in the USSR, coincide with regions of race, culture, and language. So throughout the nineteenth century in Europe, nationalism

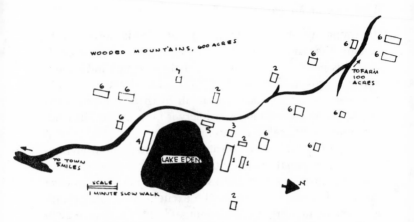

Black Mountain College (after P. Williams) 1. Study buildings 2. Shops and Laboratories 3. Exhibits and Meetings 4. Dining hall 5. Library 6. Living quarters 7. Quiet house

could be regarded as economic, cultural, and linguistic regional planning. (In contrast, the Chinese Communists seem to want to break down regional differences by transplanting whole populations.) In an advanced technology like the American, however, economic regionalism is vanishing. Doorframes for a building in Denver were manufactured on the East Coast, but people in New York eat garden vegetables from Texas: this seems idiotic, but the technology and transport warrant it, and the economy apparently demands it. We saw that Fuller refused to consider any space-age region less than the continents of the world around the North Pole. (And if we believe the writers of science fiction, as how can we not, our region is the Milky Way.) Of cultural regionalism we have little: our one distinctive region is the so-called "South," whose unity consists in oppressing Negroes to the mutual disadvantage of Negroes and whites. In fact, our striking cultural regions are precisely the metropolitan centers, New York, the Bay Area, perhaps Chicago; and vast cities do require a kind of regional planning of traffic, taxation, and civic function.

Geophysical regions do exist spectacularly in our country. It is pathetic if the esthetic advantages of our unique landscapes, of our coasts, plains, subtropics, mountains, river valleys and deserts, cannot make us a more various America than we are getting. In our history, the Americans have thrown away one of our most precious heritages, the Federal system, a system of *political* differences of regions, allowing for far-reaching economic, legal, cultural, and moral experimentation—as the La Follettes experimented in Wisconsin, the Longs in Louisiana, as Sinclair tried in California. (Or as Alberta, Canada tried out Social Credit.) This was the original idea of our system. When the fathers gave up the leaky Articles of Confederation for the excellent aims of the Preamble, they were not thinking of a land with an identical gas station, Woolworth's, and diner at every crossroads; with culture canned for everybody in Hollywood and on Madison Avenue; and with the wisdom of local law dominated by the FBI.

The TVA

The improvement of the Tennessee Valley by the Tennessee Valley Authority started with a single natural resource: a flow of water with a head of as much as 5000 feet, caused by precipitation of up to 80 inches over a region touching half a dozen states. Previous to the Authority, part of this flow was developed for electric power and the fixing of nitrogen, for munitions and later for fertilizer. The Authority was empowered to expand this into a multiple-use handling of the waterway: a system of dams, locks, reservoirs and channels for power, navigation, and flood-control. But this at once involved the improvement of the watershed itself to assure steady flow and good volume of storage; so the Authority turned to forestation, prevention of erosion, and improvement of cultivation.

At this point a profound change occurred in the idea.

The concept of a multiple-use enterprise is familiar in business; the sum of different kinds of products, by-products, and services make possible a capital investment which for any one of them would be unprofitable; this is the case in most extractive and refining industries. What was unique in the TVA was the decision to spread the benefits of one part of the enterprise, the waterway, to the farmers of the whole region without specific evaluation of the cash outlay and return, the principle being just "the general social benefit." This decision, this principle, was possible because it is the immediate products of the waterway, not their cash equivalents, that the farmers need: electric power, water, and fertilizer extracted or processed by industrial electricity. That is, there was an absolutely new fund of wealth produced by the project and directly contributing, without middlemen or a high cost of distribution, to the expanding benefits of the project. It might seem that this direct contribution and immediate specific value of the products was a

The Tennessee Valley

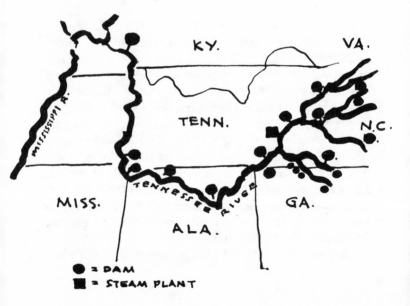

● = DAM
■ = STEAM PLANT

mere convenience of bookkeeping; but indeed, it was just this that has made the whole a model of integrated regional planning, naturally expanding and seizing useful opportunities, relatively free from the profit nexus of society as a whole.

An enterprise in which the productive combinations of nature play a major part—we have cited the instance of the symbiotic farm—has a powerful and generous capitalist indeed! Nor is it easy to keep its books in double entry. That here was something unique has been proved by the violent subsequent lawsuits concerning the "yardstick" for setting a competitively fair price for power that is being distributed, (1) As a social benefit; and (2) As necessary for the perfection of the valley improvement.

The natural benefits of the regional improvement have made themselves felt far outside the region, in controlling flood and in moderating the effects of drought a thousand miles away. How to price that? And without question, if the industrial use of the region were exploited by the electro-metallurgical and other electric industries, pursuing the same social policy of free expansion, the economic effect would be enormous throughout the nation. The necessity, for efficiency, of setting up a power grid over a wide area alters the economy of the private power companies adjacent. Also, a picturesque region sensibly developed becomes by definition a place for recreation.

But the most telling proof of the force of such a naturally integrated plan is the continual emergency of ingenious inventions, in an expanding activity supported by a steady surplus of directly useful resource. Along with the invention of a new fertilizer came an ingenious machine for depositing seed and fertilizer in one operation; along with the consequent introduction of diversified crops and dairying, came electric processes for both quick-freezing and dehydration.

An architectural invention developed by the Authority deserves special mention: the section trailer-houses, a kind of moving town, adapted to the migration of thousands of skilled workers from one construction site to another. These

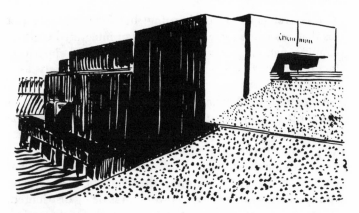

TVA: "severely decorative functionalism"

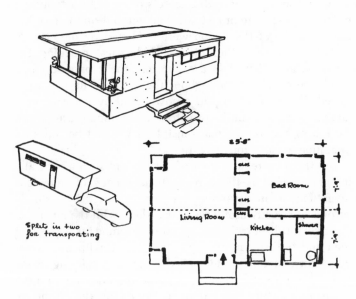

Splits in two
for transporting

25'-6"

Bed Room

Living Room

Kitchen

Shower

TVA: a portable house

had a meaning and beauty superior to the design of the main structures themselves, in which the planners of the Authority take inordinate pride but which, as Fritz Gutheim naïvely boasts, are "the architecture of public relations." (The style of severely decorative functionalism.)

To sum up, let us quote from the description of the TVA in the final report (1934) of the National Resources Planning Board: "There is a broad technical integration of the specific tasks assigned to T.V.A., which have raised fundamental issues of social policy and have involved planning on a scale unusual in the United States. To begin with, the effort to set up a well-managed, low-cost, self-supporting system of power production necessitates the integrated development of the Tennessee River. The prevention of soil-erosion is necessary to prevent the dams from silting up within a century. But erosion is a prblem in its own right. To prevent it, a program of afforestation and public works must be undertaken, and large areas turned from plow crops to grass. This cannot be done without experimental work in the development of phosphate fertilizers. To further this transformation and to develop the agricultural potential of the region, provision has been made for encouraging the cooperative movement. To find a market for the potential power has involved lowering the selling price of power for domestic use and the lowering of the price of electric appliances through the Electric Home and Farm Authority.

"The work of the T.V.A. has dealt with large social issues, some of which involve substantial modifications of the existing institutional structure of the country. Most fundamental of all is a decision of Congress to establish public ownership and operation of hydroelectric works in the Valley; the demonstration of the economy of social service in this field may foreshadow a broad change from private to public operation of utilities in the United States. The elimination of private enterprise by the T.V.A. and the extension of rural electrification carries with it a reconsideration of the criterion of profitability. There is a difficult decision, involving social policy, that must be made with regard to the

purchase price of privately owned distributing systems. In
connection with the program to prevent soil-erosion it is
deemed necessary to redefine property rights. These and
other examples may be cited as large social changes implicit
in the execution of the technical tasks assigned to the
T.V.A."

This necessity of overriding political and economic boundaries, and of following the functional relationships within
the region, comes from the original decision to exploit nature
directly rather than after it has been more or less fixed in
commodities and capital, whether in a profit system or in
the framework of a national plan determined from some
political center. Nature proves to have novel potentialities;
new problems arise, and new solutions are found in hardly
suspected natural resources. Following natural subject matter, human inventiveness.

But of course this process soon comes to its limits; the
institutions of society reassert themselves. It is after all only
a natural region.

Norris Dam

PART II

Three Community Paradigms

Introduction

Values and Choices

Such are some great plans of the past century that variously emphasize the relation between the means of livelihood and the ways of life. Now let us make a new beginning and collect our conclusions for our own problems in this book: How to make a selection of modern technology? How to use our surplus? How to find the right relation between means and ends?

We have chosen to present our thoughts in the form of three community models of our own. Given the complex and incommensurable factors of the subject, this seems to us the simplest as well as the liveliest method of presentation: to give typical important value-choices as if they were alternative programs and plans. None of these is presented as our own point of view. In fact, we should probably prefer to live in the second or middle scheme, and we don't make much effort to conceal our bemusement about the first, which is similar to New York in 1960. Nevertheless, these three models are not plans, they are analyses; they refer to no site; they have no style, which comes only in building something concrete; and most important, there is no population that purely makes these alternative choices as we present them. People in fact want a mixture of the three, in varying proportions depending on their traditions and circumstances.

Gunnar Myrdal, a great sociologist and a philosophic man, has said:

> Value premises must be explicitly stated and not hidden as tacit assumptions . . . Since incompatible valuations are held in society, the value premises should ideally be given as a number of sets of alternative hypotheses.

119

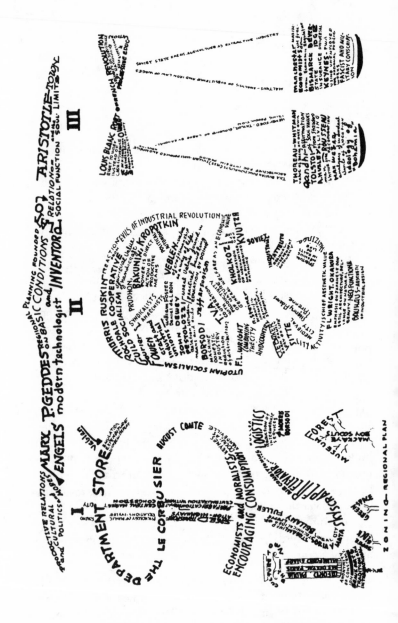

Bibliography for three ways of life today

This is exactly what we try to do. We present three alternative models of choices with regard to technology, surplus, and the relation of means and ends, and we ask what each formula gives us in economics, politics, education, domestic standards, popular and high culture, and other functions of the community. These are regional schemes for:

A. *Efficient Consumption.*
B. *Elimination of the Difference between Production and Consumption.*
C. *Planned Security with Minimum Regulation.*

The Need for Planned Luxury Consumption

American production requires a vast tribe of advertisers to boost the standard of living: this buys up the goods on the home market and allows for profitable reinvestment. The standard is very high but even so it often fails in important areas, sometimes in automobiles, sometimes in eggs. No doubt we ought to give away more of our goods abroad and so increase the world standard. But it is an era when other lands are, or are hastening to become, advanced technologies, and given the speed with which machine tools are multiplied and machine skills are learned, we can easily envisage the day when we won't be able to give anything away, we will *have* to use it ourselves.

Our productivity is of course immensely higher than the actual production. During the 30's, it is figured, we ran at much less than 50%, yet supported a luxury leisure class of a million and ten million unemployed of whom none starved except by the error of a social agency. During the war, production was nearer 90% of capacity (though inefficient, as emergency production must be), and many millions of the economically unemployed, in the armed services, enjoyed the use of such luxury commodities as tanks, bombers, heavy artillery, and warships. Since the war, though the standard has leaped higher, the productivity is again tightly checked.

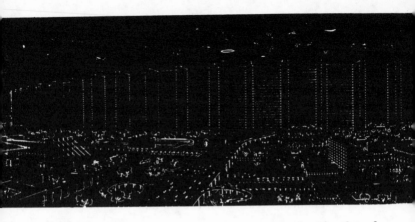

View from the University zone: the means of livelihood in the center

J. K. Galbraith has beautifully shown that, for all the ideology, no real attempt is made to improve production but only to maintain employment and protect present investment. A solution would be to slacken off the whole enterprise and cut down the hours of labor, but most of the workers (if we may judge by their union demands) do not want the leisure, they want the goods and the "fringe benefits."

How to run nearer to capacity and also use up the goods? There has to be a planned production and a planned consumption to match it. The first is an economic problem, and government economists sometimes work at it—for us it is not pressing except in emergencies of war or depression. But the second, predominantly psychological, problem is always with us; it is left to the free lances of Madison Avenue. The results are never noble or gorgeous, often absurd, and sometimes immoral. (For instance, a typical expedient that the advertisers have hit on in despair is to give away $64,000 to bright children and truckloads of electrical appliances to suburban ladies. But this creates in everybody's mind an incompatible clash of values, between the hard money that you work for and the soft money that is given away—as prizes or stipends for TV appearances down to fringe benefits and social insurance. Eric Larrabee has stated it as a rule that the less hard you work for it, the more you are paid.)

Adam Smith said: "Consumption is the sole end and purpose of production; and the interest of the producer ought to be attended to only so far as may be necessary for promoting that of the consumer. The maxim is so perfectly self-evident that it would be absurd to attempt to prove it." As a general moral maxim, it is certainly false: in this book we shall demonstrate two contrary purposes of production, as a way of life (Chapter 6) and as a means of freedom (Chapter 7). But for a market capitalism or a planned production expanding by the reinvestment of profits—and this is what Smith was thinking of—his maxim is still axiomatic, *if* the economy is to be good for anything at all. For such an economy, matching the planning of production and the efficient use of labor, we have to turn a concept of Veblen's upside down and speak of "Efficient Consumption."

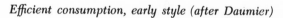

Efficient consumption, early style (after Daumier)

When Veblen set up as the opposite poles of economic morality the "instinct of workmanship" and "conspicuous waste," he was thinking of an economy of scarcity. Laboriousness, interest in technique, absence of superstition, and the other virtues of engineers seemed to him necessary to produce plenty, equality, and freedom; whereas combativeness, classical education, and gambling guaranteed insecurity and kept the masses in their place. But the fact is that now for at least three decades it has been not scarcity of production, but the weakness of the consumption attitudes of emulation, ostentation, and sheer wastefulness, that has depressed the productivity which is the economist's ideal. Only the instincts unleashed by war have sufficed, under modern conditions, to bring economic salvation.

So our first model is an analysis of how men can be as efficiently wasteful as possible. It is a city founded on the premises of the official economics, whether of Adam Smith or Keynes; yet it seems also to meet the moral demands of the New Yorkers.

CHAPTER 5

A City of Efficient Consumption

The Metropolis as a Department Store

We must have a big community. For it is mass production that provides the maximum quantity of goods. Yet, for a productivity expanding by the reinvestment of capital, the most efficient technical use of machinery is self-defeating: the product is standard and once it has been universally distributed, there is no more demand. (For instance, a great watch manufacturer has said, in a private remark, that in a year he could give everybody in the world a cheap durable watch and shut up shop.) One solution is to build obsolescence into the product; this, it is alleged, is being done in some industries, but it is morally repugnant. More morally tolerable, and psychologically exciting, is to have a variety of styles and changing fads. So we require a combination of mass production, variety of style, and changing fads. This means a big population: let us say, to mass-produce requires a large market (100,000), and if there are 50 styles of each kind, we come to 5 million.

But why must the big population be concentrated in metropoles? First, of course, on purely technical grounds, for efficient distribution and servicing under conditions of mass production. (Under conditions of a quasi-domestic industry, the situation is otherwise.) We must refer here to the well-known fact that, during the last 70 years, although the percentage of farmers has steadily dwindled, the percentage of workers in manufacturing has hardly increased; the great gain has been in the workers in "services." A part of these are teachers, doctors, social workers—groups playing a major role in any consumption economy; but the greater part are in transport, city services, etc. These have only an indirect role in production, and therefore countervene our principle of the simplest relation of means and ends.

OCCUPATIONS—July 1956

(U. S. Bureau of Census) (*figures in millions*)

Factory Operatives	12½
Craftsmen	9
Common Labor	4
Clerical	9
Administrative	7* ⎫
Sales	4* ⎬ = 11
Farm	8
Professional and Semi-Professional	5½* ⎫
Service	5½* ⎬ = 13
Domestic	2 * ⎭

Everyone agrees there is a great increase in services. Are the starred items "services"?

Another figure from the Dept. of Labor: In 1919 there were 25 million "goods-producing workers." Today the figure is about the same. But "service employees" have increased from 15 millions in 1919 to over 30 millions in 1958.

To minimize non-productive and non-consumptive services we must have (1) Concentration of production and market, and (2) Planning of the city to minimize services.

We can come to the same conclusion of big cities by moral and psychological considerations. There is the possibility, as we shall presently show, of making machine production a way of life and immediate satisfaction; but when, as in the case we are now discussing, the tendency of production is toward quantity and sale on a profitable market, the possibility of satisfaction in the work vanishes. The ideal of work then becomes, as we see in the current demands of labor unions, pleasant and hygienic working conditions, short hours at the task, and high wages to spend away from it. The workman wants to hasten away wealthy, unimpaired in health and spirits, from the job that means nothing to the home, the market, the city, where are all good things. This tendency is universal; it does not depend on machine industry; for we see that the farm youth, once it is acquainted with the allures of city life and city money, flocks to the city year after year in 50% of its strength.

(It is also true that the colorless routine of machine production produces an opposite flight impulse: to escape the artificial framework of society altogether. This appears as an impulse toward suburbs and Garden Cities, but it is really an impulse toward the open country and the woods. So in our city we must plan for the polar opposites: the pleasures of the metropolis and the escape to the open country.)

The goods must be on display; this is possible only in a big city. And the chief motivation to get those goods for oneself is not individual, the satisfaction of instinct and need; it is social. It is imitation and emulation, and these produce a lively demand. At first, perhaps, it is "mass comforts" that satisfy city folk—these show that one belongs; but then it is luxuries, for these give what Veblen used to call the "imputation of superiority," by which a man who is not in close touch with his own easygoing nature can affirm himself as an individual, show he has style and taste, and is better. All this can take place only in a big city.

Aristotle said long ago, "The appetite of man is infinite"—it is infinitely suggestible.

The heart of the city of expanding effective demand is the department store. This has been seen by many social critics, such as Charlie Chaplin, Lewis Mumford, and Lee Simonson.

Here all things are available according to desire, and are on display in order to suggest the desire.

The streets are the corridors of the department store.

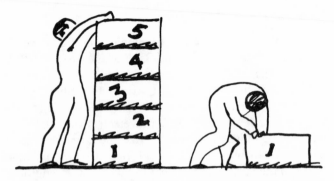

Every worker today produces five times more than his grand-father did in 1880 (National Bureau of Economic Research).

Then let us sum up this preliminary program for the city:
1. A population of several million as the least economic (regional) unit.
2. Production and market concentrated to minimize distribution services.
3. The city concentrated to minimize city services.
4. Work and life to center around the market.
5. Morality of imitation and emulation.
6. Decoration is display.
7. Close by the open country, for full flight.

On the Relation of Production and Consumption

The community is zoned according to the acts of buying and using up. Now there are four classes of goods.

First are the goods which have been produced and are consumed in the enjoyment of them. These are all the things to be bought in a great department store, creature comforts of the body and spirit. Creaturely necessities styled to be comforts and luxuries, so they are desired as well as

needed, by the addition of titillation, form and color, novelty, and social imputation—the necessities that are perpetually necessary again and whose satisfaction wears out and must be renewed. And such, for the spirit, are the popular arts; they serve for entertainment and distraction, and to communicate current news, feelings, and fads. These spiritual demands are perpetually renewed; for instance, an illustrated magazine a week old is worthless. Such, negatively, are the running repairs of medicine and social work. These products, physical comforts, popular arts, and medicine, that are periodically necessary and wear out, are the most marketable goods. (It is only in a vicious society that the more habitual needs, of form and truth, passion and sociality, and virtue, seem to be equally marketable.)

Morley's theorem: the trisections of the angles of a triangle intersect in an equilateral triangle.

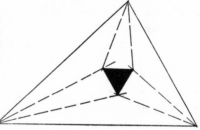

Then the second class of goods are those which have been produced but are not consumed in the enjoyment. These are all the monuments of form and truth in the arts and sciences. Essentially not marketable at all, but their current presentation according to the prevailing fashion is marketable. Such goods are often wrongly called the culture of society, but it is rather the popular arts and journalism which are the culture, the principle of social cohesion. The great arts are humane, nearer to nature than culture: their social dress—their popularity in their day—soon becomes dated and "period." To signalize this difference, just as their enjoyment does not consume them, so their production is often distinguished by the name of creation.

The third class of goods, those which are consumed in the enjoyment but are not produced by men, belong to nature immediately; they are the underlying and indispensable factors in any community: social and sexual intercourse, domestic life, ultimately everything pertaining to the primary environment of parents, children, friends. It is daily life that is consumed but not produced; people draw on their own resources, to wear them out and to renew them for a while. It is here that the things bought at the market are used, for self-assurance and prestige, and because of lack of individual initiative; yet in the end the principle of the community in this zone must be spontaneous demand and naturally given resources, as in the family and the elementary schools, relatively free from the suggestion and display which is the whole culture of the market itself. (Thus, small boys must play sandlot ball; it is only in a vicious society that they are tricked, by unscrupulous clothiers and publicity-mad parents, into putting on the uniforms of the Little League.) Apart from this freedom, the internal springs of demand dry up.

Lastly, there are the goods which are neither produced nor consumed: the stream of life itself and the permanent things of nature, recurring not by conscious reaching out but by unchanging laws of reproduction, growth, and death. They are created literally, and are not consumed but grow and die. For these, the standard of living is not comfort and luxury, but subsistence. Rural life, in relative poverty, reproduces itself the most. In the community, this zone belongs essentially to the children and adolescents, and to those adults who are temporarily spent. The adults in their vigor are concerned mainly with culture, status, and pleasure.

The four kinds of goods give us the four zones of the city.

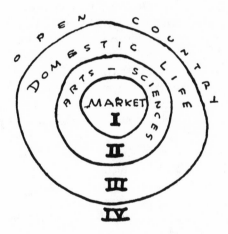

A Metropolitan Region

We turn to the selection of industries. Now in general every external activity is planned on the principle of efficiency, the efficiency of means to achieve ends, where the means are somewhat external arrangements and the ends are more internal satisfactions.

Bird's-eye view

We shall see in our next chapter that if we consider the means of life also part of a man's internal time of life, the principle of efficiency becomes blurry; industries are selected on moral and psychological grounds. And in the 7th chapter, where we are concerned with freedom from control, we shall not ask much about the ends at all, but simply reduce the means (of subsistence) to a minimum. But in this present discussion, a metropolitan region of efficient luxury, we can concentrate on quite definite ends: how the wealth of the external scene can by suggestion and gratification fill life—and then efficiency is strictly a technical problem; how to produce the most with the least waste in non-productive services, transport, middlemen between producer and consumer. The principle of selection of industries is therefore the most possible—light and heavy manufacture and agriculture—up to the point where concentration is threatened by wasteful intermediaries.

Taking an average of five major cities (1957) as our figure, we find that by the scientific use of existing techniques, the work of 4½ million in light and heavy manufacture, trade, and administration, and their residence, entertainment, education, and culture—and all this with a spaciousness, where it is relevant, that is twice that of the best American standard—can be concentrated in a circle five miles in radius: a New York City that could lie on Staten Island. And around this inner circle, a zone for the gardening of vegetables sufficient for the entire population and worked by the citizens themselves, spreads less than twenty miles additional. The beginning of open forest can be sometimes 5, and never more than 25, miles from the center of the city.

For the sake of exposition, let us choose an economy somewhat like New York but with a greater proportion of heavy industry. Then we select the following livelihoods:

> Light manufactures, such as clothing and electrical appliances
> Heavy manufacturing, such as motor cars or ships
> Business administration and advertising
> A market, for the region and the nation
> Entertainment, for the nation
> Agriculture, for the region

The location of these businesses and industries is as follows. All merchandising, both regional and national, is in the center where the buyers gather near the terminals and elevators. Administration is centralized for convenience of communication. Light manufacture is in the center, where

Size of cities

FIVE CITIES - 1957
POPULATION and density per mile

NEW YORK	7,800,000	24,000
Tokyo	5,400,000	33,500
Moscow	5,100,000	51,000
Berlin	3,400,000	9,800
Chicago	3,000,000	19,200

its parts, already processed, can arrive and its exports leave from the central terminal. Heavy manufacture is on the outskirts, shipping by rail or truck. Truck gardening is included because its farmers can live in the city, on the basis of the conservative figure of one acre to feed twenty-five; but dairy farming is excluded; requiring one acre for five, it spreads too far for convenient working by the city folk. The local airport, passenger and freight, is in the center. (Long distance airport is at the outskirts.)

The zoning of the community functions of the metropolis, however, is according to the fourfold relation of production and consumption, as analyzed above: (1) The market, populated by workers, traders, and transients, and including hotels, restaurants, popular arts, and terminals; (2) Arts, sciences, and the university; (3) Domestic life, consisting of neighborhoods, with their residences, elementary schools, hospitals, shops, and garages; and (4) Open country: a vacationland for all, with camps for children and junior colleges for adolescents, among the forest preserves.

The Center;
Theory of Metropolitan Streets and Houses

Our proposal to place the entire work and market center under one roof, as one immense container, once seemed extreme and sensational; today it is not unusual and reflection will show that it is logical.

In existing great cities, which have large buildings and congested downtown centers, there are always three simultaneous systems of streets: the through highways (skyways, freeways, etc.); the old city-streets (avenues and side-streets); and the corridors of the large buildings. The through highways, coming more and more to be elevated or tunneled, carry the main stream of traffic uptown and to places outside the city. It is wrongly thought that by increasing these highways and so facilitating approach to the center, the traffic congestion can be thinned out; but in the

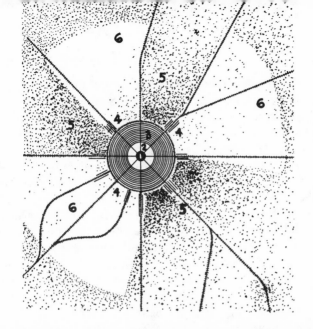

Regional plan: 1. Market, light industry, offices, entertainment, hotels, and terminals 2. Culture, universities, museums, zoo 3. Residences, schools, hospitals 4. Heavy industry, terminals, long distance airports 5. Forest preserves, vacationland 6. Agriculture.

Log cabin to air-conditioned cylinder

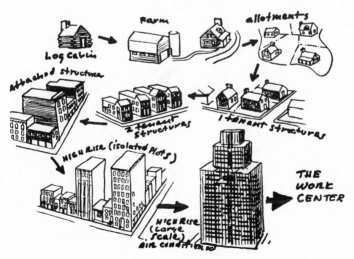

end all the highways must pour their cars into the city streets, for it is these streets that join building to building, and it is at a particular building, and not at downtown as a whole, that the motorist wants to arrive. Once he has arrived at the building, however, he is quite willing to leave his car (if there were a place to leave it) and go indoors and use the corridors and elevators of the building to bring him to the office or department where he has business.

Under these conditions, of motor traffic and increasingly large buildings, the city-streets become pointless: they are useless for traveling and unfit for walking and window shopping. At the same time they cover 35% of the ground space and require the most costly and elaborate of the city services: paving, traffic control, cleaning, snow removal, etc. For servicing, they are neither properly in the open (so that snow, e.g., could be simply pushed aside) nor yet are they indoors (protected). These streets, then, serve as the perfect example of the intermediaries that waste away the social wealth and health.

So we make of the many large buildings one immense container. The intermediary streets vanish. They have merged with the internal corridors, which are now trans-figured and assume the functions of promenade and display which the street performed so badly—in summer too hot, in winter too cold. (What we propose is no different from the arcades or souks of hot North African countries.) And the through driveways now carry out their function to the end, bringing passengers and goods directly to stations in the container, without two speeds and without double loading for trucks and trains. This makes simple sense.

Let us look at it from the opposite term of the relation, the building arrived at. The concept of a self-contained "house" has two extremes: at the one extreme is the private house on its land, with which it maintains a productive relation; at the other is the large building, containing many activities within its walls. In between we can trace a con-tinuous series from the allotment garden to the two-family and semi-detached house to the tenement and the sky-scraper. Each point of this series answers best to particular conditions. But the pell-mell of buildings, large and small, in a congested downtown district loses every function whatsoever: the streets are no longer an environment; the buildings must be lighted and ventilated in disregard of them; the real environment is increasingly distant; yet because of the crowding and competition for street space, and the need to have a dim illumination left for the streets, the interiors cannot expand to their proper spaciousness. Therefore we proceed to the extreme of merging the buildings.

The gain in concentration is enormous, amounting to several hundred per cent. Even more remarkable is the saving in construction and servicing: in the entire downtown district there is now only one exterior wall and rigid

A street floor in the air-conditioned cylinder; one mile in diameter, air-conditioned, brightly lit, flexible space; transportation vertical, horizontal and diagonal; continuous interior show window. The perimeter is for hotels and restaurants, air-conditioned but naturally lighted.

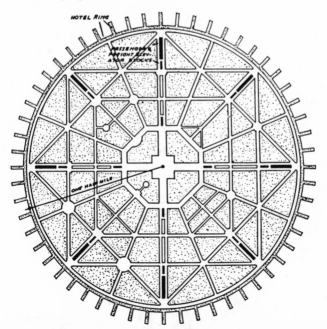

roof to lose heat and cold. Lighting, ventilation, cleaning, and so forth can be handled on a uniform system.

In a market economy, the concentration of display and convenience creates social wealth. We have the spaciousness and brilliance of a great department store.

The center, then, is the container of the work, the public pleasures, and the market. Its population, at the busy hours, is about two and a half million. It is zoned as follows. The materials and products of light manufacturing go via the freight routes in the basement or the cargo planes that alight on the roof: the heart of industry is about in the middle. Business and administrative offices are in the upper and outer regions. The lower stories—most immediately available to the citizens who come by bus or car—house the stores and popular entertainments. In the outer envelope and in projecting spokes, with natural light and a good natural view, are the hotels and restaurants, opening out, on the ground floor, into the park of the university. Convenient to all is the roof airport and the basement levels of parking and transit.

Advertising

In planning and decoration the center is a department store. Everywhere, in every corridor, as at a permanent fair, are on display the products that make it worthwhile to get up in the morning to go to work, and to work efficiently in order to have at the same time the most money and the most leisure.

The genius of this fair is advertising. Advertising has learned to associate with the idea of commodities the deepest and most various instincts of the soul. Poetry and painting are advantageous to sales; the songs of musicians are bound inextricably to soaps and wines. The scientific curiosity of men is piqued by industrial exhibits. The sentiments of brotherhood and ambition both make it imperative to buy something; sexual desire even more so. Also, the fear

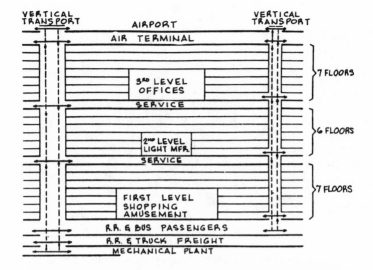

A section through the air-conditioned cylinder: twenty stories of continuous rentable area without courts or yards; four stories of passenger terminals for air, railroad, and bus; one story for terminals for light manufacture, with deliveries direct to vertical transportation; the lowest level contains the cylinder service (heat, cold, etc.)

of loneliness or sexual failure make it impossible to omit to buy something. Mother love is a great promoter of sales. In this manner the integral man is involved in the economy.

Once upon a time advertising was a means of informing the public that such and such a commodity was for sale and where it could be got. Later, advertising became competitive, persuasion to buy such and such a brand rather than any other brand. But in our time, among the largest companies—and especially among those who have something to sell, that is, perhaps, not absolutely necessary—the competitive use of advertising is no longer the chief use; indeed these companies ("partial monopolies") confine themselves to the same amount and type of advertising in order not to compete to the death. But the chief use of advertising, in which the rivals cooperate, is to suggest to a wider public the need for the product which is not, per-

Street scene in the cylinder: always perfect shopping weather

haps, absolutely necessary. It is this new departure in advertising that gives one confidence in the economic feasibility of an expanding productivity. But such advertising must be given the right atmosphere in which to breathe.

The University

The next zone is the university, extending in a mile-wide ring around the center: this consists of theaters, opera houses, museums, libraries, lecture halls and laboratories of liberal arts and sciences, and everything that belongs to these. It is the region of the things created by man or discovered in nature, and not consumed in the enjoyment.

This region, as we witness in our great cities and their universities, is the field of a deadly internecine strife: between those who would integrate these classical creations and discoveries very closely into the culture of the center, and those who fear that this integration corrupts everything into hogwash. Thus, there is a great museum in New York City which alternates the exhibition of severe modern classics of painting with the exhibition of advertising posters. The problem comes up as a problem of location: whether, for instance, to locate among the humanities of the university such popular humanities as higher merchandising, or to locate these in the center as trade schools. There is no question, also, that the classics of art and science do enter into the nexus of exchange (e.g., paperbound books), and could be made to do so even more. On the other hand, such books are *not* consumed in the enjoyment, they do not have an expanding production, and to exploit them is pennywise, pound-foolish. Careless popularization of the classics injures the solid economic value of illustrated weeklies. Humane education is necessary to keep things going at all, but too much of it makes people too simple.

Provision is made in the park for thrashing out these and similar problems. There are outdoor cafés and places for

Plan of the university: C, The Center 1. Natural history, zoos, aquariums, planetarium 2. Science, laboratories 3. Plastic arts 4. Music and drama

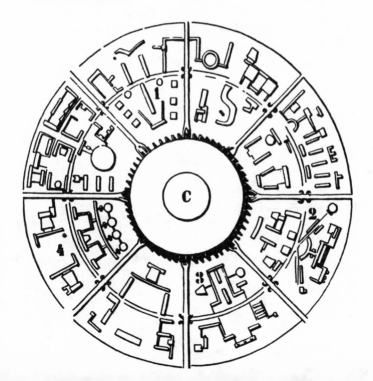

dancing, accessible to the transients from the hotels as they emerge from the center.

Within the center, style and decoration present no difficulty. They are whatever is fashionable this season. To illustrate them for our purposes we need merely imitate what is highly correct in the spring of 1960 (taken from *The New Yorker* magazine). Such imitation would not be good decoration, for decoration requires an intuitive popular sympathy, hard to keep up year after year unless one is in the business, but it would be *like* good decoration.

But the style of the university is a different matter, and a thorny problem. What is the "future" style of something that is only an analytic model? Therefore we cannot show any illustration of the elevation.

Neighborhoods

In modern community plans that take any account at all of amenity, there is always an idea of neighborhood, neighborhood blocks, as opposed to the endless addition of the city gridiron or of isolated dwellings in the suburbs. This is because it returns to the human scale and face-to-face acquaintance. And in the city of efficient consumption, too,

Along a radial highway in a residential zone

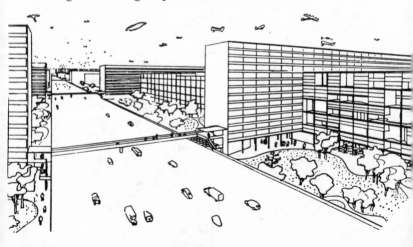

the neighborhood is the primary unit of emulation and invidious imputation.

We demonstrate this as follows. It is in the end unsatisfactory and indelicate to emulate, or to impute economic inferiority to, one's family and friends; on the other hand, to do so with total strangers is pointless. Therefore, at least for domestic display, the unit of emulation and so forth must be the neighborhood. Residents of one's neighborhood take notice, judge one's clothes, see that the lawn is clipped; they are not so well known that one is embarrassed to show off to them; they do not know us well enough to see through us.

The neighborhood must be a mixture of classes. Each class must be well enough represented to fortify each family's security and to allow for the more subtle forms of imputation that are practiced among persons invited to one another's homes. But the juxtaposition of different classes is necessary in order to practice the grosser forms of emulation, which keep people on their toes. (For intraclass emulation is more likely to keep people on each other's toes, considering that we make a personal as well as economic judgment of our friends.) In our fortunate city, there is no danger to the juxtaposition of even extreme classes, since all have goods and need not despair of getting more.

We need, then, a neighborhood of a certain size, perhaps a few thousand. So we typically arrange the residences in neighborhood blocks of about 4000 population, in a continuous apartment house around an open space of up to ten acres. Each block has its shops, tennis courts, nurseries, elementary schools, where the neighbors may commune and vie. It is not desirable for these neighborhoods to generate important local differences, for all must take their standards from the mass-produced peculiarities on sale at the center.

This residential population is composed largely, up to 40%, of older persons. This is the inevitable result of two trends—increased longevity under improved medicine and the flight of young families to the suburbs. Our city has the

Residences: the style of the whole is anonymous; the cell individualized.

maximum of medicine, urbanism and wealth. Correspondingly, we have the perfection of a valetudinarian environment: protected from the elements, air-conditioned, with smooth transportation, rapid service, all arranged not to excite the weak heart or demand agility from unsteady feet. The neighborhoods contain clinics, hospitals, and nursing homes.

It is an environment of space, food, sunlight, games, and quiet entertainment, whose standard requirements, largely biological and psychological, are agreed on by everybody.

Apartments

The idea of feudal Anglo-Saxon law that "a man's home is his castle" came to refer to the situation of the gentry, in which the house and its land maintained a productive relation of comparative self-sufficiency. Take away the land and the idea is seriously weakened. And as community domestic services—light, gas, water—invade the house, its architectural meaning vanishes. Finally, such services can be provided efficiently only in an apartment house. The apartments are increasingly mass-produced and the houses become larger.

The problem is how to establish a contrary movement, to restore family choice and freedom in the new architectural conditions. The reality of a house is the space within (Bruno Zevi). Let us restrict the imposition of the architect to its minimum function, the provision of efficient shelter and services. We then provide for each family an empty shell without partitions and (for the rich) two stories high, completely serviced with light, conditioned air, water, and so forth, through the columns of the building as in an office building. Hitherto architectural practice has provided not only such a serviced shell but also the imitation of a house, with plan and fundamental decoration complete, partitions, paneling, balcony, etc. But these parts have no structural nor technical necessity and belong to private taste, need, or caprice; they need not be standard.

Street plan in a residential district

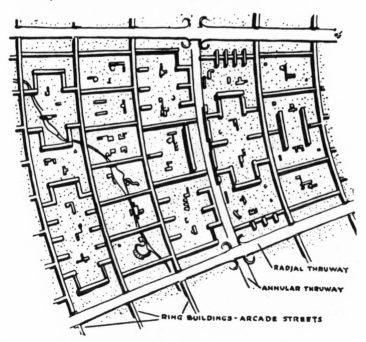

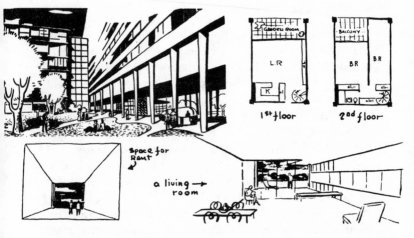

Residential space: at the left, a corner of a residential block showing an arcade and its local shops; above it a pneumatic delivery system operating from the City-Center (for packages up to a yard in diameter). The rest shows a typical apartment space, rented as a bare loft and made livable and/or expensive according to individual taste and/or fancy.

Open Country

The last zone is the open country. This appears suddenly, not straggling into being amid outlying homes, factories, and cultivated fields, as if marking the exhaustion of the energies of the city, but full of the ambivalent energy of society, as nightmare and waking are parts of the same life. For a dream (but which is the dream, the city or the woods?) is not a temperate expression of the repressed desires of the day, but a strange flowering of them, often too rich to bear. In this vacationland there is exchanged for the existence where everything is done for you, the existence where nothing is done for you. You have, who venture there, the causality of your own hands, and the gifts of nature.

These conditions are hard for city folk and they are finally moderated—after, say, 50 miles, three-quarters of an hour

by car or 15 minutes by helicopter—into the imitation wild-
ness of state parks and the bathos of adult camps.

Perhaps in this moderate and forgetful forest can be initiated the procreation which is impossible to initiate by
urban standards.

Children are here conveniently disposed of in camps during the summer season.

It seems wise to locate in the open region the age of
adolescence, and its junior colleges. Here is space for its
unconventional moods and violent play. This group, more
than any other, wants to be alone with its contemporaries in
small communities; it is impatient of the old and young,
meaning anybody five years older or two years younger.

As civilization becomes more complex and demanding,
the problem of psychological initiation into culture becomes
more pressing. Now the small child, brought up in the
metropolis, remembers, rather unconsciously than consciously, the elegance of his mother at home—still elegance to
him, even when it is contrived of cheap cosmetics. But
the adolescent, given to rebellion, is encouraged, by a more
animal existence in the open country. And we know that
as his longings settle into habitual desires, it is the environment of adult achievement that seems attractive to him;
he has been away from it, and "nothing increases relish
like a fast." In hundredfold strength the impressions of
childhood have him in grip. Then the university, the school
of adults both young and old, glorifies the values of the
city in its popular humanities, and in its pure humanities it
provides the symbols of reasonable sublimation for those
who come by destiny to see through the machinery.

Such then are the four zones of the city.

Politics

There is no direct political initiative to make either central or neighborhood policy. For the expanding economy
exists more and more in its nice interrelationships and is

run by a corporation of technologists, merchandisers, and semi-economists as directors. Periodic elections are like other sales campaigns, to choose one or another brand name of a basically identical commodity.

An existence of this kind, apparently so repugnant to craftsmen, farmers, artists, or any others who want a say in what they lend their hands to, is nevertheless satisfactory to the mass of our countrymen, so it must express deep and universal impulses. These probably center around what Morris Cohen used to call the first principle of politics, inertia; that is, that people do not want to take the trouble to decide political issues because, presumably, they have more important things on their minds.

But in fact the most powerful influence that people exercise, and would exert even more powerfully in a city of efficient consumption, is the economic choice to buy or not to buy a product and to be employed in this or that factory or office. We are not speaking of such strenuous efforts as boycotts or strikes, but of the delicate pressures of the market, which in a market of luxuries and a production of full employment profoundly effect particular brands, without disturbing the system as a whole. In our society even great captains of industry and princes of merchandise who, one would have thought, would have freedom to do it their own way, cannot step out of line. A famous manufacturer, for instance, is said to have believed in the transmigration of souls, but he was not allowed by his public relations department to proselytize to this belief because it might seem odd to potential customers. Everybody who has a penny can influence society by his choice, and everybody has, in principle, a penny.

Thus, there is direct social initiative neither from above nor below. This explains the simply unbearable quality of façade or "front" in American public thought: nobody speaks for himself, it is always an Organization (limited liability) that speaks.

Wish fulfillment of an efficient consumer

Carnival

But now comes—what is proper to great cities—a season of carnival, when the boundaries are overridden between zone and zone, and the social order is loosed to the equalities and inequalities of nature. "A holiday," said Freud, "is a permitted, rather than a proscribed, excess; it is the solemn violation of a prohibition."

Yet it is not necessary to imagine any astonishing antics and ceremonies of carnival; for as society becomes more extensively and intensively organized in its means of livelihood, any simple gesture occurring in the ways of life is already astounding, just as in Imperial Germany to walk across the grass was a revolutionary act. By day-to-day acquiescence and cooperation, people put on the habit of some society or other—whether a society of consuming goods or some other makes no difference, so long as there are real satisfactions. Meantime, submerged impulses of excess and destruction gather force and periodically explode in wild public holidays or gigantic wars. (There is also occasional private collapse.)

The carnival, to describe it systematically, would be simply the negation of all the schedules and careful zoning that are full of satisfaction in their affirmation. No one can resist a thrill when a blizzard piles up in the streets and the traffic stops dead. The rumor of a hurricane brings out our child souls and much community spirit.

Describing the Saturnalia of the Roman Empire, an old writer gives the following particulars: "During its continuance, the utmost liberty prevailed: all was mirth and festivity; friends made presents to each other; schools were closed; the Senate did not sit; no war was proclaimed, no criminal executed; slaves were permitted to jest with their masters, and were even waited on at table by them. This last circumstance was probably founded on the original equality between master and slave, the latter having been, in the early times of Rome, usually a captive taken in the war or an insolvent debtor, and consequently originally the equal of his master . . . According to some, the Saturnalia was emblematic of the freedom enjoyed in the golden age, when Saturn ruled over Italy."

During the carnival in the city of efficient consumption a peculiar incident sometimes occurs. At one of the automatic cafeterias in the center where, on the insertion of a coin, coffee and cream pour from twin faucets and neatly fill a cup to the brim, this machine breaks down—all nature conspiring in the season of joy—and the coffee and cream keep flowing and do not stop, superabounding, overflowing the cup, splashing onto the floor; many cups can be filled from the same source. (This is not so absurd, it happened to our mother once in Minneapolis.) Then gathers a crowd and a cheer goes up as they indulge in inefficient consumption.

Installment debts are forgiven. And with the pressure of installment-payments removed, people swing to the opposite extreme and don't work at all: they fail to provide even for

the day's necessities and begin to eat up the capital investment. They consume the reserve piled up on the market.
The economy apparently ceases to expand (but its shelves
are merely being cleared for new fashions).

In the factories, basketball courts are rigged up, emblematic of the sit-down strikes that occurred in America in 1935.

The people are not really idle, but only economically so.
They are feverishly preparing and launching immense
floats: works of imperishable form—there is a classic tradition of the forms—but made of the most perishable materials
possible, papier mâché, soap, ice. These floats, after pa-
rading through the streets, are destroyed without residue:
the paper is pushed into bonfires, toasts a moment, and
leaps up in a puff of flame, through which the deathless
form seems to shine one last moment after its matter has
vanished. The soap is deluged by hoses and dissolves in
lather and iridescent bubbles; and the forms of ice are left
to melt slowly away in the brilliant darts of the sun.

At home people engage in rudimentary domestic industry
and in the imitation of self-sufficient family economy. It is
customary for each family to engage in a little agriculture
in the closet and grow mushrooms, the *fungus impudicus*
that springs up in the night like the phallus. Women devote
themselves to the home-manufacture of a kind of spaghetti
or noodles, and from all the windows in the residential
neighborhoods can be seen, hanging from poles and drying
in the sun, such fringes of spaghetti or noodles. Wood fires
are lit from sticks of furniture going out of fashion, and
meals are prepared of noodles or spaghetti with mushroom
sauce.

It is during this week that there is the highest hope of
engendering children, not to have to rely exclusively on
the immigration of the tribes beyond the forest.

From the forest invade mummers in the guise of wolves
and bears. These wolves and bears (students from the
junior colleges) prowl and dance among the monuments
of urbanism. They sniff along the superhighways by moon-

light, and they browse among the deserted rows of seats in cinemas, where candy is left for them to eat. By their antics, they express astonishment at these places.

Thus, finally, can be observed the dread sight that poets, ancient and modern, have seen in visions: of wolves prowling by moonlight in the deserted streets of cities. So now—when the coffee and cream have soured among the legs of the tables, and the shelves are bare; when only the smoke is arising from the pyres and the bubbles have collapsed, and there are puddles where stood the statues of ice; and when the city folk are asleep, gorged with their meal and with love; the streets are deserted; now by moonlight come these wolves, rapidly up the wrong side of the streets and prowling in empty theaters where perhaps the picture (that the operator neglected to turn off) is still flickering on the screen, to no audience.

Next day, however, when the carnival is over and the rubbish is efficiently cleared away by the post-carnival squad, it can be seen that our city has suffered no loss. The shelves have been cleared for the springtime fashions; debtors have been given new heart to borrow again; and plenty of worn-out chattels have been cleaned out of the closets and burnt.

Carnival

CHAPTER 6

A New Community:

The Elimination of the Difference between Production and Consumption

Quarantining the Work, Quarantining the Homes

Men like to make things, to handle the materials and see them take shape and come out as desired, and they are proud of the products. And men like to work and be useful, for work has a rhythm and springs from spontaneous feelings just like play, and to be useful makes people feel right. Productive work is a kind of creation, it is an extension of human personality into nature. But it is also true that the private or state capitalist relations of production, and machine industry as it now exists under whatever system, have so far destroyed the instinctive pleasures of work that economic work is what all ordinary men dislike. (Yet unemployment is dreaded, and people who don't like their work don't know what to do with their leisure.) In capitalist or state-socialist economies, efficiency is measured by profits and expansion rather than by handling the means. Mass production, analyzing the acts of labor into small steps and distributing the products far from home, destroys the sense of creating anything. Rhythm, neatness, style belong to the machine rather than to the man.

The division of economy into production and consumption as two opposite poles means that we are far from the conditions in which work could be a way of life. A way of life requires merging the means in the end, and work would

153

have to be thought of as a continuous process of satisfying activity, satisfying in itself and satisfying in its useful end. Such considerations have led many moralist-economists to want to turn back the clock to conditions of handicraft in a limited society, where the relations of guilds and small markets allow the master craftsmen a say and a hand in every phase of production, distribution, and consumption. Can we achieve the same values with modern technology, a national economy, and a democratic society? With this aim, let us reanalyze efficiency and machine production.

Characteristic of American offices and factories is the severe discipline with regard to punctuality. (In some states the law requires time clocks, to protect labor and calculate the insurance.) Now no doubt in many cases where workers cooperate in teams, where business is timed by the mails, where machines use a temporary source of power, being on time and on the same time as everybody else is essential to efficiency. But by and large it would make little difference at what hour each man's work began and ended, so long as the job itself was done. Often the work could be done at home or on the premises indifferently, or part here part there. Yet this laxity is never allowed, except in the typical instances of hack-writing or commercial art—typical because these workers have an uneasy relation to the economy in any case. (There is a lovely story of how William Faulkner asked M-G-M if he could work at home, and when they said, "Of course," he went back to Oxford, Mississippi.)

Punctuality is demanded not primarily for efficiency but for the discipline itself. Discipline is necessary because the work is onerous; perhaps it makes the idea of working even more onerous, but it makes the work itself much more tolerable, for it is a structure, a decision. Discipline establishes the work in an impersonal secondary environment where, once one has gotten out of bed early in the morning, the rest easily follows. Regulation of time, separation from the personal environment: these are signs that work is not a way of life; they are the methods by which, for better or worse, work that cannot be energized directly by personal concern can get done, unconfused by personal concern.

In the Garden City plans, they "quarantined the technology" from the homes; more generally, we quarantine the work from the homes. But it is even truer to say that we quarantine the homes from the work. For instance, it is calamitous for a man's wife or children to visit him at work; this privilege is reserved for the highest bosses.

Reanalyzing Production

In planning a region of satisfying industrial work, we therefore take account of four main principles:

1. A closer relation of the personal and productive environments, making punctuality reasonable instead of disciplinary, and introducing phases of home and small-shop production; and vice versa, finding appropriate technical uses for personal relations that have come to be considered unproductive.

2. A role for all workers in all stages of the production of the product; for experienced workers a voice and hand in the design of the product and the design and operation of the machines; and for all a political voice on the basis of what they know best, their specific industry, in the national economy.

3. A schedule of work designed on psychological and moral as well as technical grounds, to give the most well-rounded employment to each person, in a diversified environment. Even in technology and economics, the men are ends as well as means.

4. Relatively small units with relative self-sufficiency, so that each community can enter into a larger whole with solidarity and independence of viewpoint.

These principles are mutually interdependent.

1. To undo the present separation of work and home environments, we can proceed both ways: (a) Return certain parts of production to home-shops or near home; and

(b) Introduce domestic work and certain productive family-relations, which are now not considered part of the economy at all, into the style and relations of the larger economy.

(a) Think of the present proliferation of machine-tools. It could once be said that the sewing machine was the only widely distributed productive machine; but now, especially because of the last war, the idea of thousands of small machine shops, powered by electricity, has became familiar; and small power-tools are a best-selling commodity. In general, the change from coal and steam to electricity and oil has relaxed one of the greatest causes for concentration of machinery around a single driving-shaft.

(b) Borsodi, going back to the economics of Aristotle, has proved, often with hilarious realism, that home production, such as cooking, cleaning, mending, and entertaining has a formidable economic, though not cash, value. The problem is to lighten and enrich home production by the technical means and some of the expert attitudes of public production, but without destroying its individuality.

But the chief part of finding a satisfactory productive life in homes and families consists in the analysis of personal relations and conditions: e.g., the productive cooperation of man and wife as it exists on farms, or the productive capabilities of children and old folk, now economically excluded. This involves sentimental and moral problems of extreme depth and delicacy that could only be solved by the experiments of integrated communities.

2. A chief cause of the absurdity of industrial work is that each machine worker is acquainted with only a few processes, not the whole order of production. And the thousands of products are distributed he knows not how or where. Efficiency is organized from above by expert managers who first analyze production into its simple processes, then synthesize these into combinations built into the machines, then arrange the logistics of supplies, etc., and then assign the jobs.

As against this efficiency organized from above, we must

try to give this function to the workers. This is feasible only if the workers have a total grasp of all the operations. There must be a school of industry, academic and not immediately productive, connected with the factory. Now let us distinguish apprentices and graduates. To the apprentices, along with their schooling, is assigned the more monotonous work; to the graduates, the executive and coordinating work, the fine work, the finishing touches. The masterpiece that graduates an apprentice is a new invention, method, or other practical contribution advancing the industry. The masters are teachers, and as part of their job hold free discussions looking to basic changes.

Such a setup detracts greatly from the schedule of continuous production; but it is a question whether it would not prove more efficient in the long run to have the men working for themselves and having a say in the distribution. By this we do not mean merely economic democracy or socialist ownership. These are necessary checks but are not the political meaning of industrialism as such. What is needed is the organization of economic democracy on the basis of the productive units, where each unit, relying on its own expertness and the bargaining power of what it has to offer, cooperates with the whole of society. This is syndicalism, simply an industrial town meeting. To guarantee the independent power of each productive unit, it must have a relative regional self-sufficiency; this is the union of farm and factory.

3. Machine work in its present form is often stultifying, not a "way of life." The remedy is to assign work on psychological and moral as well as technical and economic grounds. The object is to provide a well-rounded employment. Work can be divided as team work and individual work, or physical work and intellectual work. And industries can be combined in a neighborhood to give the right variety. For instance, cast glass, blown glass, and optical instruments; or more generally, industry and agriculture, and factory and domestic work. Probably most important, but difficult to

conjure with, is the division in terms of faculties and powers, routine and initiation, obeying and commanding.

The problem is to envisage a well-rounded schedule of jobs for each man, and to arrange the buildings and the farms so that the schedule is feasible.

4. The integration of factory and farm brings us to the idea of regionalism and regional relative autonomy. These are the following main parts:

(a) Diversified farming as the basis of self-subsistence and, therefore, small urban centers (200,000).

(b) A number of mutually dependent industrial centers, so that an important part of the national economy is firmly

The town and its environs: 1. City squares. 2. and 3. Diversified farms accommodating all the children and their schools (the parents who work in the squares will generally live in the inner belt) 4. Industrialized agriculture and dairying 5. Open country, grazing, etc.

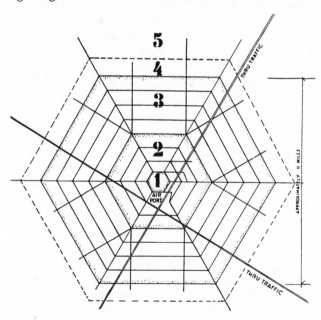

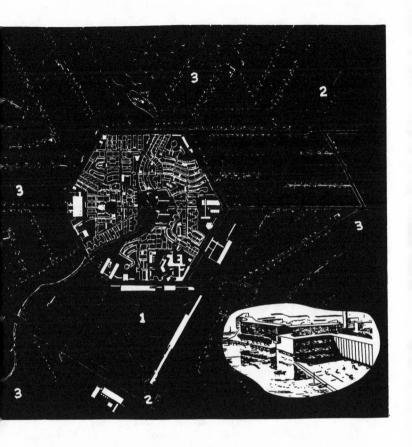

*The city squares and farms within bicycle distance: the principle
of the plan is that, except for the nuisance factories on the outskirts, none of the community or domestic functions is zoned in
isolation. Thus the squares will be formed by libraries, factories,
dwellings, stores, schools, restaurants, etc., as function, appearance, and community sentiment dictate (cf. Printing Square,
p. 163). 1. Airport and interregional market 2. Express highways,
green belt, and nuisance factories 3. Four-acre farms, urban
parents' dwellings and elementary schools. The peripheral roads,
bordering the hexagon of city squares and serving the local
automobile and truck traffic, pass under or over the express roads
or connect with them by ramps.*

controlled. (The thought is always to have freedom secured by real power.)

(c) These industries developed around regional resources of field, mine, and power.

Diversified farmers can be independent, and small farms have therefore always been a basis of social stability, though not necessarily of peasant conservatism. On the other hand, for the machines now desirable, the farmer needs cash and links himself with the larger economy of the town.

The political problem of the industrial worker is the reverse, since every industry is completely dependent on the national economy, for both materials and distribution. But by regional interdependence of industries and the close integration of factory and farm work—factory workers taking over in the fields at peak seasons, farmers doing factory work in the winter; town people, especially children, living in the country; farmers domestically making small parts for the factories—the industrial region as a whole can secure for itself independent bargaining power in the national whole.

The general sign of this federal system is the distinction of the local regional market from the national market. In transport, the local market is served by foot, bicycle, cart, and car; the national market by plane and trailer-truck.

(Now all of this—decentralized units, double markets, the selection of industries on political and psychological as well as economic and technical grounds—all this seems a strange and roundabout way of achieving an integrated national economy, when at present this unity already exists with a tightness that leaves nothing to be desired, and an efficiency that is even excessive. But we are aiming at a different standard of efficiency, one in which invention will flourish and the job will be its own incentive; and most important, at the highest and nearest ideals of external life: liberty, responsibility, self-esteem as a workman, and initiative. Compared with these aims the present system has nothing to offer us.)

A Schedule and Its Model

TYPICAL SCHEDULE OF ACTIVITIES FOR MEMBERS OF A COMMUNE
(*numerals equal months*)

Basic Work	Master Workman	Apprentice Workman	Farmer	Farm Family	Ages 6 to 14	Ages 15 to 18
Factory	8(a)	6				1
Industrial Agriculture		3(d)	2(d)	√		1
Diversified Agriculture			{ 8	√	√	
Domestic Industry			{ 8	√(e)		1
Formal and Technical Learning		2(b)				1(b)
Technical Teaching	1(b)		1(b)			
General Education					√	5
Study and Travel						2(f)
Individual Work (c)	2					
Unscheduled (g)	1	1	1	1	√	1

Notes on the Schedule

(a) The factory work of the master workman and workwoman includes executive and fine work.

(b) The time of technical education runs concurrently with the working period.

(c) Graduate work at one's own time and place could be in a traveling trailer or country cottage; could comprise designing, drafting, assemblage of hand-assembled wholes (e.g., radios or clocks), finishing operations (lens-grinding), etc.

(d) Master farmwork in industrial agriculture includes super-vision and maintenance and is divided cooperatively to spread over the year. The more mechanical work at peak seasons is done by the factory apprentices.

(e) Farm-family industry includes the making of parts for the factories, cooperation with industrial agriculture (e.g., field kitchens), educational care of boarding city children.

(f) The spread of activity of the youth over many categories, i ıcluding two months of travel, gives them an acquaintance with the different possibilities.

(g) Activity at one's own fancy or imagination—vocational, avocational, recreational, etc.

(√) Activities engaged in as occasion arises.

A Piazza in the Town

With us at present in America, a man who is fortunate enough to have useful and important work to do that is called for and socially accepted, work that has initiative and exercises his best energies—such a man (he is one in a thousand among us) is likely to work not only very hard but too hard; he finds himself, as if compulsively, always going back to his meaningful job, as if the leisurely pursuits of society were not attractive. But we would hope that where every man has such work, where society is organized only to guarantee that he has, that people will have a more good-humored and easygoing attitude. Not desiring to get away from their work to a leisure that amounts to very little (for where there is no man's work there is no man's play), people will be leisurely about their work—it is all, one way or another, making use of the time.

Now, the new community has *closed squares* like those described by Camillo Sitte. Such squares are the *definition* of a city.

Squares are not avenues of motor or pedestrian traffic, but are places where people remain. Place of work and

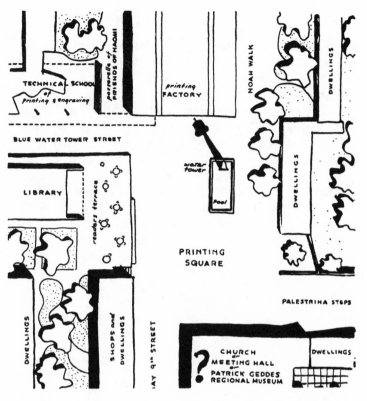

A square in the town: integration of work, love and knowledge

home are close at hand, but in the city square is what is still more interesting—the other people.

The easygoing leisure of piazzas is a long simple interim, just as easygoing people nowadays are often happiest on train trips or driving to work, the time in-between. Conscience is clear because a useful task will begin at a set time (not soon). The workers of the new community give themselves long lunchtimes indeed. For, supposing ten men are needed on a machine or a line for four hours' work: they arrange to start sometime in midafternoon, and where should they find each other, to begin, but in the piazza.

On one side of the piazza opens the factory; another entrance is a small library, provided with ashtrays. As in all other squares, there is a clock with bells; it's a reminder, not a tyrant.

The leisure of piazzas is made of repetitive small pleasures like feeding pigeons and watching a fountain. These are ways of being with the other people and striking up conversations. It is essential to have outdoor and indoor tables with drinks and small food.

There is the noise of hammering, and the explosions of tuning a motor, from small shops a little way off. But if it's a quieter square, there may be musicians. Colored linen and silk are blowing on a line—not flags but washing! For everything is mixed up here. At the same time, there is something of the formality of a college campus.

A busy square

A quiet square

Another face of the piazza is an apartment house, where an urban family is making a meal. They go about this as follows. The ground floor of the building is not only a restaurant but a foodstore; the farmers deliver their produce here. The family cooks upstairs, phones down for their uncooked meat, vegetables, salad, and fixings, and these are delivered by dumbwaiter, cleaned and peeled—the potatoes peeled and spinach washed by machine. They dress and season the roast to taste and send it back with the message: "Medium rare about 1845." The husband observes, unfortunately for the twentieth time, that when he was a student in Paris a baker on the corner used to roast their chickens in his oven. Simpler folk, who live in smaller row houses up the block, consider this procedure a lot of foolishness; they just shop for their food, prepare it themselves, cook it, and eat it. But they don't have factory jobs: they run a lathe in the basement.

The main exit from the square is almost cut off by a monument with an inscription. But we cannot decipher the future inscription. The square seems enclosed.

In the famous piazzas described and measured in all their

asymmetry by Camillo Sitte, the principal building, the building that gives its name to the place, as the Piazza San Marco or the Piazza dei Signori, is a church, town hall or guild hall. What are such principal buildings in the squares we are here describing? We don't know.

The windmill and water tower here, that work the fountain and make the pool, were put up gratuitously simply because such an ingenious machine is beautiful.

A Farm and Its Children

Let us rear all the children in the natural environment where they are many and furnish a society for one another. This has an immense pedagogic advantage, for the business of the country environment is plain to the eyes, it is not concealed in accounts and factories. The mechanism of urban production is clear to adult minds; the nature of farm production is not much clearer to the adults than to the children of ten or eleven.

Integrating town and country, we are able to remedy the present injustice whereby the country bears the burden of rearing and educating more than its share of the population, then loses 50% of the investment at maturity. (And then the cities complain that the youth have been educated on rural standards!) If the city children go to the country schools, the city bears its pro rata share of the cost and has the right to a say in the policy.

The parents who work in the city live in small houses on nearby farms: that is home for the children. But when they leave for work, the children are not alone but are still at home on the farm. Some such arrangement is necessary, for it is obvious that we cannot, as the urban home continues to break down, be satisfied with the pathos of crèches, nursery-schools, and kindergartens.

To the farmers, the city families are the most valuable source of money income.

The best society for growing children, past the age of

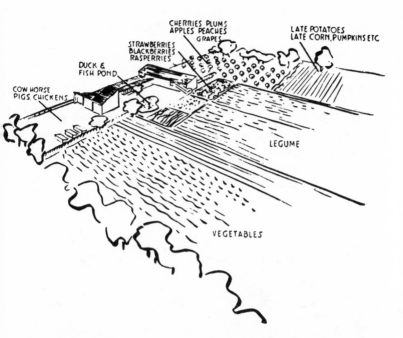

Disposition of farm production. The principle of the diversified farm is symbiosis, with a minimum of artificial fertilizer; city sewage, enriched by the products of the farm, is piped back to fertilize the land.

total dependency, is other children, older and younger by easy grades. It is a rough society but characterized at worst by conflict rather than by loving, absolute authority. These children, then, no longer sleep with their parents, but in a dormitory.

From quite early, children are set to work feeding the animals and doing chores that are occasionally too hard for them. Perhaps urban sentiment can here alleviate the condition of farm and city children both.

Everybody praises diversified farming as a way of life. Yet the farm youth migrate to the city when they can. (Just as everybody praises lovely Ireland, but the young Irish leave in droves.) This is inevitable when all the advertised social values, broadcast by radio and cinema, are urban values. It is universally admitted that these values are claptrap; but they are more attractive than nothing. To counteract this propaganda, the farm-sociologists try to establish a social opinion specifically rural, they revive square dances and have 4-H clubs and contests, organized by the farmers' collectives and cooperatives.

But is it necessary for "farm" and "city" to compete? All values are human values.

The yard; the house is built of prefabricated and local materials.

First floor: large space for gathering and food, a room for domestic industry, a room for the children's play and study near the work room and the farmyard. Second floor: sleeping

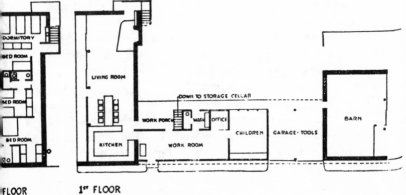

Interior of the gathering-space and view from the road. A combination of handwork and prefabrication. The painting (after Mondrian) is not placed against a painted wall.

Regional and National Economy

The large number of diversified farms means, on the one hand, that the region is self-subsistent, but on the other that the farmers have little crop to export outside the region. Their cash comes, however, from the city market, from domestic industry, from some industrial agriculture, and from housing the city folk. If farmers have a specialized crop, such as grapes or cotton, it is processed in the town. All this guarantees a tight local economy.

Now, even apart from political freedom, such a tight local economy is essential if there is to be a close relation between production and consumption, for it means that prices and the value of labor will not be so subject to the fluctuations of the vast general market. A man's work, meaningful during production, will somewhat carry through the distribution and what he gets in return. That is, within limits, the nearer a system gets to simple household economy, the more it is an economy of specific things and services that are bartered, rather than an economy of generalized money.

"Economy of things rather than money"—this formula is the essence of regionalism. The persons of a region draw on their local resources and cooperate directly, without the intermediary of national bookkeeping with its millions of clashing motives never resoluble face-to-face. The regional development of the TVA, brought together power and fertilizer for farms, navigation and the prevention of erosion, the control of floods and the processing of foods, national recreation, and in this natural cooperation it produced a host of ingenious inventions. All of this (in its inception) was carried on in relative autonomy, under the loose heading of "general welfare."

The kind of life looked for in this new community depends on the awareness of local distinctness, and this is also the condition of political freedom as a group of industries and farm cooperatives, rather than as a multitude of abstract votes and consumers with cash.

Yet every machine economy *is* a national and international economy. The fraction of necessary goods that can be produced in a planned region is very substantial, but it is still a fraction. And this fact is the salvation of regionalism! For otherwise regionalism succumbs to provincialism—whether we consider art or literature, or the characters of the people, or the fashions in technology. The regional industrialists in their meeting find that, just because their region is strong and productive, they are subject to wide circles of influence, they have to keep up.

Refinement

Let us try to envisage the moral ideal of such a community as we are describing.

In the luxury city of consumers' goods, society was geared to an expanding economy—capital investment and consump-

---

SOME ELEMENTARY PRINCIPLES
FOR THE
MORAL SELECTION OF MACHINES

1. **Utility** (Functionalist beauty)

2. **Transparency of Operation**

   A. Repairability by the average well-educated person (Freedom)

B. Constructivist beauty

3. **Relative independence of machine from non-ubiquitous power**

4. **Proportion between total effort and utility** (Neo-Functionalist beauty)

tion had to expand at all costs, or even especially at all costs. In the third community that we shall describe in this book, "maximum security, minimum regulation," we shall find that, in order to achieve the aim of social security and human liberty, a part of the economy must never be allowed to expand at all.

But in this present, middle-of-the-road, plan there is no reason why the economy either must expand or must not expand. Every issue is particular and comes down to the particular question: "Is it worthwhile to expand along this new line? Is it worth the trouble to continue along that old line?"

This attitude is a delicate one, hard for us Americans to grasp clearly: we always like to do it bigger and better, or we jump to something new, or we cling. But when people are accustomed to knowing what they are lending their hands to, when they know the operations and the returns, when they don't have to prove something competitively, then they are just in the business, so to speak, of judging the relation of means and ends. They are all efficiency experts. And then, curiously, they may soon hit on a new conception of efficiency itself, very unlike that of the engineers of Veblen. When they can say, "It would be more efficient to make it this way," they may go on to say, "And it would be even *more* efficient to forget it altogether."

Efficient for what? For the way of life as a whole. Now in all times honorable people have used this criterion as a negative check: "*We* don't do that kind of thing, even if it's convenient or profitable." But envisage doing it positively and inventively: "Let's do it, it becomes us. Or let's omit it and simplify, it's a lag and a drag."

Suppose that one of the masters, away on his two months of individual work, drafting designs for furniture, should, having studied the furniture of the Japanese, decide to dispense with chairs. Such a problem might create a bitter struggle in the national economy, one thing leading to another.

The economy, like any machine economy, would expand,

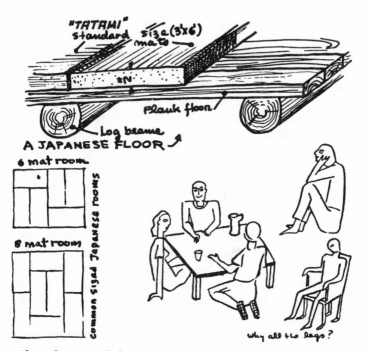

Chairs kept us off the drafty, muddy floor—but if we don't have mud floors and do have radiant heating—why chairs?

for it creates a surplus. It would expand into refinement. The Japanese way is a powerful example. They cover the floor with deep washable mats and dispense with chairs and dispense with the floor. It is too much trouble to clutter the room with furniture. It is not too much trouble to lavish many days' work on the minute carving on the inside of a finger pull of a shoji. They dispense with the upholstery but take pains in arranging the flowers. They do not build permanent partitions in a room because the activities of life are always varying.

When production becomes an integral part of life, the workman becomes an artist. It is the definition of an artist that he follows the medium, and finds new possibilities of expression in it. He is not bound by the fact that things have always been made in a certain way, nor even by the fact that it is these things that have been made. Our industrialists—even International Business Machines—are very much concerned these days to get "creative" people, and they make psychological studies on how to foster an "atmosphere of creativity"; but they don't sufficiently conjure with the awful possibility that truly creative people might tell them to shut up shop. They wish to use creativity in just the way that it cannot be used, for it is a process that also generates its own ends.

Notes on Neo-Functionalism: the Ailanthus and the Morning-Glory

In the Introduction to this book, we called this attitude neo-functionalism, a functionalism that subjects the function to a formal critique. The neo-functionalist asks: Is the use as simple, ingenious, or clear as the efficient means that produce it? Is the *using* a good experience? For instance, these days they sell us machines whose operation is not transparent and that an intelligent layman cannot repair. Such a thing is ugly in itself, and it enslaves us to repairmen.

There is one abuse of present-day production, however, that is not only ugly and foolish but morally outrageous, and the perpetrators should be ostracized from decent society. This is building obsolescence into a machine, so it will wear out, be discarded, and replaced. For instance, automobile-repair parts are now stocked for only five years, whereas previously they were stocked for ten. Does this mean that the new cars, meant to last a shorter time, are cheaper? On the contrary, they are more expensive. Does it mean that there are so many new improvements that there is no point in keeping the older, less efficient models running? There are no such improvements; the new models are characterized merely by novel gimmicks to induce sales— just as the difficulty of repair and the obsolescence are built in to enforce sales.

Neo-functionalists are crotchety people, for they are in love with the goddess of common sense, and the way we do things catches them by the throat. They take exception

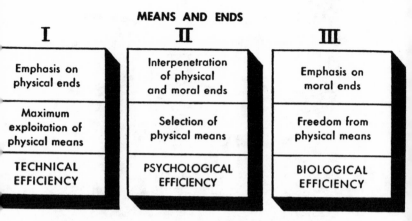

MEANS AND ENDS

I	II	III
Emphasis on physical ends	Interpenetration of physical and moral ends	Emphasis on moral ends
Maximum exploitation of physical means	Selection of physical means	Freedom from physical means
TECHNICAL EFFICIENCY	PSYCHOLOGICAL EFFICIENCY	BIOLOGICAL EFFICIENCY

A neo-functionalist analysis of the three paradigms

to much that is universally accepted, because it doesn't add up; they stop to praise many things universally disregarded, such as the custom of sitting on slum stoops and sidewalks, with or without chairs: Park Avenue does not provide this amenity. To a neo-functionalist, much that is insisted on seems not worth all that bother, and he is often easygoing; his attitude is interpreted as laziness, but he sees no reason to be busy if he is not bored. He praises the ailanthus.

Of all trees and shrubs it seems to be only the locust and especially the ailanthus that flourish of themselves in the back alleys and yard-square plots of dirt that are the gardens of Manhattan Island. They bloom from the mouths of basements. But the maple saplings and the elms that are transplanted there at large expense and are protected from pests with doses of a nauseating juice, languish and die in that environment of motor fumes and pavements.

Should our native city not, out of simple respect and piety, exalt the ailanthus to be our chief ornamental scenery, and make places for it everywhere? For the ailanthus loves *us* and thrives in our balance of nature. Our city is rich enough, it could become elegant enough, to flaunt a garden

Backyard, New York City

of native weeds. There is everywhere a prejudice against the luxuriating plantain weed, which as abstract design is as lovely as can be. Why should not this weed be raised to the dignity of a grass—it is only a matter of a name—and then carefully be weeded in, in rows and stars, to decorate the little sidewalk plots?

The Rivers of New York

Trained in the New Commune, the neo-functionalist mentions also the ludicrous anomaly of New York's bathing-places. During the heat of summer tens of thousands of Manhattanites daily travel from two to three hours to go swimming and boating on far-off shores. Many millions of dollars were spent in developing a bathing place no less than 40 miles from midtown Manhattan, and this place—it is the darling of our notorious Park Commissioner—has been connected with the city by remarkable highways on which at peak hours the traffic creeps at four miles an hour, while the engines boil.

Meantime the venturesome poor boys of the city swim daily, as they always have, in the Hudson River and the East River—under the sidelong surveillance of usually reasonable police; it is quite illegal. It is illegal because the water is polluted. No strenuous effort is made by the Park Commissioner to make it unpolluted; and the shore is not developed for bathing. Yet to the boys it seems the obvious thing to do on a hot day, to dive into the nearest water, down the hill at the end of the street, into

> *Our lordly Hudson hardly flowing*
> *under the green-grown cliffs*
> *—and has no peer in Europe or the East.*

A typical view of Manhattan, reorganized as proposed here. This is a scene along the East River, with facilities for boating, bathing, and other types of recreation. Business buildings would be confined to a narrow spine running north and south up the center of the island, near two great arterial highways.

The Museum of Art

Suppose again, says our neo-functionalist friend, that a number of mighty masterpieces of painting and statuary were decentralized from the big museum and placed, one in this neighborhood church (as in Rome one encounters astounded, *Moses*), and one on this fountain in a local square, wherever there is a quiet place to pause. A few of the neighbors would come to have a friendly and perhaps somewhat proprietary acquaintance with their masterpiece. Are they not to be trusted so close to the treasure?

One cannot help but think of Florence that has come down to us not as a museum city (like Venice), but as a bustling modern town, yet still a continuous home for those strange marble and bronze monsters of the Renaissance, in the squares. It would be very interesting for a sociologist to study, with his questionnaires, the effect of those things on the Florentines. They have had an effect.

When there is such a work in a neighborhood, a stranger, who from afar has heard of its fame, will come to visit the local square where he would otherwise never have ventured. Then the children notice how carefully and reverently he is looking at the statue they climb on.

Nurses' Uniforms

The washing and ironing of all New York's city hospitals is to be done at a great municipal laundry. And it comes out on investigation that the great part of the work can be done by a small fraction of the labor and machinery, but the small remainder of the work requires all the rest of the labor. It is the kind of situation that puts a neo-functionalist on the alert. It is that most of the labor goes into ironing the uniforms of doctors and nurses, but especially into ironing the frilly bonnets and aprons. The washing and the flatwork is done by machine and mangle, but the frills require hand-finishing.

It's not worth it. Make the uniforms of seersucker or anything else that doesn't need ironing. Make the hats in the form of colored kerchiefs that could equally well indicate the schools from which the nurses have come.

These conclusions are offered to the city fathers who have ordered a functional laundry to be designed; but they decide that they're not practical.

The Morning-Glory

Yet our neo-functionalist friend, who is a great lover of oriental anecdotes, also approvingly tells the following story.

"In the sixteenth century, the morning-glory was as yet a rare plant in Japan. Rikiu had an entire garden planted with it, which he cultivated with assiduous care. The fame of his convolvuli reached the ear of the Taiko, and he expressed a desire to see them; in consequence Rikiu invited him to a morning tea at his house. On the appointed day

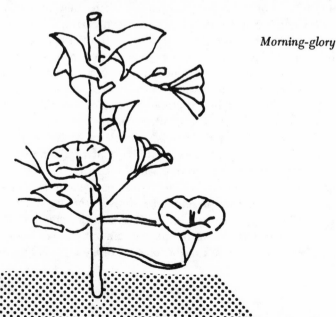

Morning-glory

the Taiko walked through the garden, but nowhere could he see any evidence of the flower. The ground had been leveled and strewn with fine pebbles and sand. With sullen anger the despot entered the tearoom, but a sight restored his humor. In the tokonoma, in a rare bronze of Sung workmanship, lay a single morning-glory—the queen of the whole garden." (Kakuzo Okakura)

The Theory of Packages

In general, when the consumption of a product is removed from its production, by the geographical distance between factory and home, by the economic distance of sale and resale up to retail, and the temporal distance between making and use, the product is encased in a series of packages. There are the shipper's crate and the wholesaler's case and the middleman's carton and the retailer's box and the waterproof, airtight cellophane wrapper that must be kept inviolate and untouched except by the ultimate eater.

These packages are the career of physical goods as a commodity, and once the last wrapper is broken, the commodity is destroyed, it is unsaleable. It has been corrupted by the moisture and air and germs of life, by the passionate fact that someone wants the thing enough to touch it rather than sell it. Economically, then, this is a sacramental moment, when a man or woman brutally breaks the wrapper and takes the bread out of circulation. (From any point of view, the insipid taste is less interesting.)

The principle of packages is a corollary of Ralph Borsodi's blanket principle that as the cost of production per unit decreases by mass production, the cost of distribution increases because of the intermediaries involved in mass distribution. From this principle he derives the paradox of prosperity and insecurity: the copiousness of commodities entails the subordination of the consumer to a vast economic machine which can become deranged in different

parts and leave him without elementary necessities. Borsodi's principle does not mean that machine production
and labor-saving devices are humanly inefficient, but only
when they become too geographically and economically
centralized. Borsodi himself is an enthusiast for domestic
machines and home industries, but there is also the possibility of a reasonably large community of integrated industrial, agricultural, domestic and cultured life, where the
efficiency of machines can be exploited without insecurity.

Time

At present, a man's time of life is also put into packages.
We speak, as the British anarchist Woodcock has pointed
out, of "lengths of time as if they were length of calico." He
concludes that the clock, the time clock that the worker
aggressively "punches," is the chief machine of industrial
exploitation, for it enables human labor to be quantified
and priced as a commodity.

This commodity-time is the time of not-life that people
step into when they take leave of their hearts, their homes,
and even their heads, early in the morning. It is the time
of a secondary environment which is, however, still loud
with the authoritative but inner and forgotten voice of

parents who seemed to wish (so children get to think) to deprive one of pleasure and ease. Especially in the morning at twenty to eight, and late in the afternoon at twenty after four, the fatherly face of the clock is frowning, deeper first on the left side, then on the right.

Advertising

Every one of the packages is printed with is own mumbo-jumbo of words.

In the nature of the case, when the consumer is far from the producer; has not ordered the production nor handled the means of it; nor estimated the cost of the means in proportion to the satisfaction enjoyed; it is necessary to *interest* him in the product, to create a want for it that has not been fired by any previous activity. (When we make or command something to be made, there are goal gradients toward the use.) Also, he must be persuaded to buy it if it is something that is, perhaps, not absolutely indispensable. All these functions are fulfilled by advertising, which draws less and less on the direct relation between the excellence of the product and the cost of its making—the word "cheap" is never used—but more and more on the comparative estimates of social opinion, emulation, fear of inferiority or not belonging. These drives require a handsome fund of insecurity to begin with.

Pictures and slogans are repeated again and again, and it is now classical theory, and perhaps even somewhat true, that repetition leads to belief and even overt action. This theory is true under certain conditions, namely that the use of words is reflex behavior, rather than an action of need, passion, invention, observation, and reflection. It is a poor use of speech, and unfortunately it does damage to English, for free poets must now take pains to use outlandish ways of speech to make sure that their words will not be taken in the meanings to which people have become accustomed, instead of relying on, and striving to reach, the meanings to which people are accustomed.

The Theory of Home Furnishings

The furniture of a home expresses, in its quantity and kind, the division of the concerns of the soul; in different community arrangements this division falls in different places.

On the principle of neo-functionalism, the place where the chief material outlay is made should give the chief satisfaction, otherwise why bother? If this rule is neglected, the material outlay becomes a dead weight, discouraging by its initial cost and even more by its continuing presence.

Now except in the woods, the chief material outlay we see about us is the public city with its services. But in America these streets, squares, and highways do not pretend to compete in satisfaction with the private homes or the theaters of fantasy. They are a dead weight on these other satisfactions. One emerges from the theater into an environment that is less exciting, and one emerges from home into an environment that is quite impersonal and uninteresting. In late medieval times, they spent no effort on the streets, but burgher and baron adorned their homes.

Let us rather take a lesson from the Greeks who were often practical in what concerned the chief end and did not complicate their means. An Athenian, if free and male, experienced in the public places, the market, the law court, the porticoes, the gymnasia, most of the feelings of ease, intimacy, and personal excitement that we reserve for home and private clubs. He lived in the city more than at home. He had for his public objects the affairs of empire, civic duties, and passions of friendship. There was no sharp distinction between public and private affairs.

On the civic places and public institutions, then, they lavished an expense of architecture, mulcted from an empire and slaves in the silver mines, that with us would be quite deadening in its pretentiousness. But the thousands of free men were at home there.

An Athenian's domestic home was very simple; it was not

an asylum for his personality. It did not have to be filled with furniture, mirrors, keepsakes, curiosa, and games.

But a bourgeois gentleman, when he is about to leave his home in the morning, kisses his wife and daughter, steps before a mirror and adjusts his tie, and then, the last thing before emerging, puts on a public face.

The most curious examples of heavily furnished homes that are the insane asylums of the spirit frozen and rejected in the city square can be found among the middle classes at the beginning of the twentieth century. And the most curious room of this most curious home was not the bedroom, the dining room, or the parlor, where after all there existed natural and social satisfactions, but the master's den, the jungle and the cavern of his reveries. In our decade, this den of nostalgic revery is in print in the stories of *The New Yorker* magazine.

Public Faces in Private Places

It is always a question whether the bourgeois den is worse or better than no private home at all, the norm of the states ancient and modern which consider men as public animals, and homes as army barracks.

But it has remained for our own generation to perfect the worst possible community arrangement, the home of the average American. This home is liberally supplied with furniture and the comforts of private life, but these private things are neither made nor chosen by personal creation or idiosyncratic taste, but are made in a distant factory and distributed by unresisted advertising. At home they exhaust by their presence—a bare cell would give more peace or arouse restlessness. They print private life with a public meaning. But if we turn to read this public meaning, we find that the only moral aim of society is to provide private satisfactions called the Standard of Living. This is remarkable. The private places have public faces, as Auden said, but the public faces are supposed to imitate private faces. What a booby trap!

Public place,
Athens

Private place,
Victorian England

A Japanese Home

"One of the surprising features that strikes a foreigner as he becomes acquainted with the Japanese house is the entire absence of so many things that with us clutter the closets and make squirrels' nests of the attic. The reason for this is that the people have never developed the miserly spirit of hoarding truck and rubbish with the idea that some day it will come into use." (Edward Morse)

"Swallows are often encouraged to build nests in the home, in the room most often used by the family. A shelf is built below the nest. The children watch the construction of the nest and the final rearing of the young birds." (Ibid.)

"One comes to realize how few are the essentials necessary for personal comfort . . . and that personal comfort is enhanced by the absence of many things deemed indispensable. In regard to the bed and its arrangement, the Japanese have reduced the affair to its simplest expression. The whole floor, the whole house indeed, is a bed, and one can fling oneself down on the soft mats, in the draft or out of it, upstairs or down and find a smooth, firm and level surface upon which to sleep." (Ibid.)

"When a tea master has arranged a flower to his satisfaction, he will place it in the tokonoma, the place of honor in a Japanese room. Nothing else will be placed near it which might interfere with its effect, not even a plant; unless there be some special esthetic reason for the combination. It rests there like an enthroned prince, and the guests or disciples on entering the room will salute it with profound bows." (Okakura)

A Japanese house is essentially one big room, divided by sliding screens as desired, for the activity of life is ever varying. Outside and inside are also open to one another.

Tokonoma in guestroom, Hachi-ishi. (after Morse)

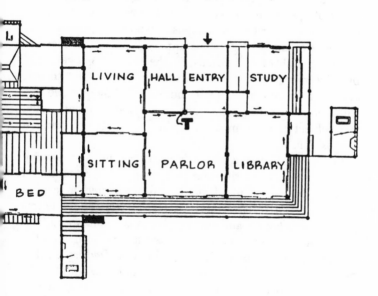

Plan of dwelling house in Tokyo: sliding screens indicated by arrows, tree trunk by T. (after Morse)

CHAPTER 7

Planned Security
With Minimum Regulation

The Sense in Which
Our Economy Is Out of Human Scale

Our economy is gigantic by the quantity and number of kinds of goods and services, but as such it is not out of human scale, for to the immense civilized population the immense quantity of goods is appropriate. The increase of useless wealth of individuals, in the form of gadgets sold by advertising, may not add to human virtue, but then it adds to folly which is equally human. The inequitable distribution of wealth, especially considered internationally, is a subject of resentment, and this is an intensely human proposition.

But we have grown out of human scale in the following way: Starting from the human goods of subsistence and luxury, the increment of profit was reinvested in capital goods in order to earn more profits, to win for the enterprisers more luxury and power; this is still human motivation. But in recent decades the result has been that the center of economic concern has gradually shifted from either providing goods for the consumer or gaining wealth for the enterpriser, to keeping the capital machines at work and running at full capacity; for the social arrangements have become so complicated that, unless the machines are running at nearly full capacity, all wealth and subsistence are jeopardized, investment is withdrawn, men are unemployed. That is, when the system depends on all the machines running, unless *every* kind of goods is produced and sold, it is also impossible to produce bread. Then an economy is out of human scale.

Social Insurance vs. the Direct Method

But elementary subsistence and security cannot be neglected by any social order; they are political needs, prior to economic needs. So the governments of the most highly capitalized states intervene to assure elementary security which is no longer the first business of the economy. And the tack they take is the following: to guarantee social security by subsidizing the full productivity of the economy. Security is provided by insurance paid in the money that comes from the operation of the whole economy. The amazing indirectness of this procedure is brilliantly exposed by the discovery of a new human "right"—as if the rights of man could be so easily amended. This is the "right to employment," failing which one gets the insurance. Full employment is the device by which we flourish; and so the old curse of Adam, that he must work in order to live, now becomes a goal to be struggled for, just because we have the means to produce a surplus, cause of all our woes. This is certainly out of human scale, yet the statesmen of America and England talk this way with absolute conviction; and anyone who spoke otherwise would be voted out of office.

The immediate result of such a solution, of insurance, social credit, or any other kind of give-away money, is to tighten even closer the economic trap. Whatever freedom used to come from free enterprise and free market—and they are freedoms which were indeed fought for with blood—is now trapped in regulation and taxes. The union of government and economy becomes more and more total; we are in the full tide toward statism. This is not a question of anybody's bad intentions, but follows from the connection of the basic political need of subsistence with the totality of an industrial economy.

So much for the indirect solution.

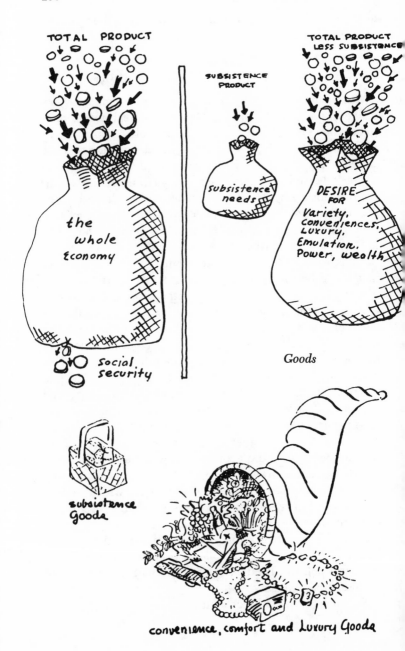

TOTAL PRODUCT

the whole Economy

Social security

SUBSISTENCE PRODUCT

subsistence needs

TOTAL PRODUCT LESS SUBSISTENCE

DESIRE FOR Variety, conveniences, Luxury, Emulation, Power, wealth

Goods

subsistence Goods

convenience, comfort and Luxury Goods

The direct solution, of course, would be to divide the economy and provide the subsistence directly, letting the rest complicate and fluctuate as it will. Let whatever is essential for life and security be considered by itself, and since this is a political need in an elementary sense, let political means be used to guarantee it. But the rest of the economy, providing wealth, power, luxury, emulation, convenience, interest and variety, has to do with varying human wishes and satisfactions, and there is no reason for government to intervene in it in any way. The divided economy has, therefore, the twofold advantage that it directly provides the essential thing that is in jeopardy, without having to underwrite something else; and it restricts the intervention of government to this limited sphere.

Up to, say, sixty years ago, more than half of the productive capacity of our economy was devoted to subsistence; subsistence could be regarded as the chief end of the economy; and whatever their own motives, most enterprisers served the subsistence market. Now, however, in the United States less than a tenth of the economy is concerned with subsistence goods. (Probably nearer a fifteenth; the exact figure would depend on what one considers an adequate minimum.) Except for the biological and political factors involved, the economic machinery could roll almost as usual though everybody were dead of starvation, exposure, and disease. When the situation is viewed in this way, one of the causes is at once clear why prosperity and surplus lead precisely to insecurity: namely, that too few people are busy about subsistence, and as we know from recent farming history, those who are busy about it try to get out of it; there's no real money in meat and potatoes.

But once the economy would be divided as we are suggesting, the very techniques of industry that, when applied incidentally to subsistence, lead to insecurity, would, applied directly to subsistence, produce it with an even smaller fraction of the social labor than at present.

Probably there are various political means by which this

small fraction of production could be effectuated, and we
will soon develop an obvious one, direct state production of
subsistence by universally conscripted labor, run as a state
monopoly like the post office or the army, but paying not
money but its own scrip, exchangeable only for subsistence
goods made by this same enterprise.

(This is a vast undertaking. It would be apparently
simpler to effect approximately the same end by using private semi-monopolistic concessionaires in the state non-
profit subsistence-business. But if indeed the production
cost is absolutely minimum and the types absolutely
standard and non-competitive, how could a private firm
profit? Further, it is intolerable, and unconstitutional, to
have to work for a private concessionaire. Therefore we prefer the state production—taking over relevant private plant
and building its own plant—because of its purity of method.
It takes subsistence *out of the economy.* Subsistence is not
something to profit by, to invest in, to buy or sell. On the
part of the consumer, it is not something to choose or reject
or contract for or exchange his labor for, but simply to
work for.)

On whatever method—and there are no doubt possibilities we have not thought of—there is one principle: to assure
subsistence by specific production of subsistence goods and
services rather than by insurance taxed from the general
economy. This involves a system of double money: the
"money" of the subsistence production and consumption
and the money of the general market. The subsistence-cer-
tificates are not money at all, for by definition a man's subsistence leaves nothing to exchange; this "money" is like
wartime ration stamps, which are likewise not legally nego-
tiable. A man's right to life is not subject to trade.

A major moral advantage of this proposal is that every
person can know that the work he does for a living is un-
questionably useful and necessary, and unexploited. It is
life itself for himself and everybody else. In our times of so
much frivolous production and synthetic demand, and the

accompanying cynicism of the producers, the importance of such a moral cannot be overestimated.

Another consequence: To everyone, but especially to the small wage earner, the separation of his subsistence, employing a small fraction of his labor time, from the demands and values of the general economy employing most of his labor time, would give a new security, a breath of freedom, and the possibility of choice. He is independent. He has worked directly for what he absolutely needs; he does not feel the pressure of being a drain on society; he does not fear that his insurance payments will cease. By the same token, people in general, including the small enterpriser, would be more fearless, for their risks are less fatal. But indeed, these things imply a change of social attitude so profound that we must think deeply about both the dangers and the opportunities.

The retrenchment of government from economic interference in the general part, again, might go very far, relaxing kinds of regulation that are now indispensable—protection of women and children, protection of unions, and so forth. For where the prospective wage earner has a subsistence independently earned, the conditions under which he agrees to work can be allowed to depend on his own education rather than on the government's coercion of the employer.

Let us sum up by contrasting the actual plans offered by present-day governments with the plan here suggested. They propose:

> Security of subsistence.
> A tax on the general economy.
> Necessity to maintain the economy at full production to pay the tax: therefore, governmental planning, pump-priming, subsidies, and made work; a still further tax, and possibly a falling rate of profit.
> Insistence on the unemployed worker's accepting the third or fourth job available, in order to prevent a continuing drain on the insurance fund.

Protection of the workers thus coerced by regulating the conditions of industry and investment.

Against this we propose:

Security of subsistence.

Loss to the industrialist and merchant of the subsistence market and a small fraction of the social labor.

Coercion of a small fraction of the social labor to produce the subsistence goods and services.

Economic freedom in all other respects.

Now financially, the choice between these two plans would depend on the comparison between the insurance and subsidies tax and the loss of labor time and market. (Unfortunately, for reasons explained below, this comparison is hard to make accurately—at least by us.) Socially and morally, however, there seems to be no comparison at all: our way is direct, simple, liberating, and allows people a quiet interim to make up their minds about things.

A History

The idea of guaranteeing subsistence by dividing the economy rather than insurance is very old and we might clarify the proposal here suggested by comparing and contrasting it with two or three of its predecessors—just as the scheme of social insurance is the heir of clerical and private charity and of the state dole. What is crucial is the relation between the subsistence economy and the general economy.

One of the earliest such ideas of modern industrial times was the communities of Robert Owen, those well-regulated squares that, starting anew in isolation, were to engage in well-rounded agriculture and machine industry, but whether with the aim of rising in the world or prospering and continuing in isolation is not really clear. For originally there seem to have been three different motives for the communities, and three distinct classes of members. First, the motive of an enlightened industrialist, ahead of both his time and ours, to make the new machine industry a humane way of life by organizing it into an all-around community, rather than by tearing labor from the countryside into wage slavery in a money economy; certain members came for this purpose, to live better. Second, the motive of a philanthropist on the poor board to provide relief for paupers by a method of self-help by which they could rehabilitate themselves at little cost to society; but in such a case, if the community succeeded, was it to continue in competition with society, or were its now capable members to filter back into the general economy? Third, the motive of a utopian pioneer to start afresh in a virgin country, away from the world of status and privilege, to establish a new society of socialism and democracy; but if that had succeeded, it would have undone the general economy.

The workshops of Louis Blanc had a more definite aim. The personnel are the unemployed who have a "right to work"; they work with capital provided by the state; and they produce goods for the general market in competition with the products of private capital. Here there is no limitation on the new economy, either of restriction to subsistence goods or of isolation, as in the Owenite communities. The scheme is, and was probably meant to be, frankly revolutionary, for how could private economy compete with a state economy that it was subsidizing by taxes on its own wealth? (Although there is evidence that the spreading of new money among the poor indeed benefited the middle class, as a modern economist would have predicted.) The fact that such an apparently explosive innovation could force its way into political acceptance proves how right Marx was when he wrote, in those years, that the specter of communism was haunting Europe. And the way in which its fires were quenched by legitimacy, by relying on the inefficiency of bureaucrats and demoralized workers, and by sabotage—so that in a moment of disillusionment the counter-revolution could strike—is a classic in political tactics and economic error.

We may also mention in this series the Homestead Act and similar plans, appropriate to societies that have large undeveloped outskirts and frontiers: free land is given to families that have failed in the general economy. The theory is that in such an open economy—especially when it is still an economy of scarcity—the increase of farmers and the development of new regions provide new markets. This is the rational notion that new wealth is to the advantage of everybody. However, when a somewhat similar farm subsidy is advanced in our own times—for instance, the loan of farm animals and machines by a government agency—the general economy is not so receptive; for the land and people rehabilitated are precisely those for which there was proved to be no use, and their products are not needed in the surplus and are not welcome as competition.

It remained for our own times, however, to hit on the ultimate possible maladjustment between public production and private production, the theory of the Works Progress Administration, as set up to combat the Depression of '29. The personnel were the unemployed, and they engaged in productive work capitalized by the state; but the New Deal had learned from the adventures of Louis Blanc not to set class against class in economic competition; therefore the products of the WPA were non-saleable. Not not-saleable in the sense that they were consumed by their producers (and that would have competed with the subsistence market), but non-saleable in kind. What products? In a state of advanced capitalism there are no such products, for everything useful is preempted as a business. Thus if, on the one hand, the WPA happened to generate something useful, like the WPA theater, it at once met the outcry of unfair competition from private enterprisers; if, on the other hand, it kept nicely within the limits of futility, it met with the charge of boondoggling. Fortunately the war turned up in different parts of the world to provide a useful non-competitive industry for everybody.

The most important variant of the WPA is the idea of using the unemployed for public works. This is a form of pump-priming. This use makes sense, but the following possibilities occur: (1) The works expand and run into competition with private enterprise, the fate of the TVA; (2) When they are social services of real value, the works' tempo and continuance ought not to depend on the supply of idle labor, but should be expertly staffed on their own; or (3) If they are made work pure and simple, then the most imposing and costly structure of society's greatest employer are restricted to the class of objects that make little difference whether or not they exist.

Conclusions from the History

As against the above, our proposal covers everybody in the society rather than a special group, the unemployed. In this it follows the plan of social insurance, which insures everyone, regardless of prospective need. Everyone is liable to a period of labor, or its equivalent, for the direct production of subsistence goods, and all are entitled to the goods.

And instead of limiting the class of persons, the limitation is set on the class of goods, subsistence goods. This kind is the most universally essential, so it is reasonable to require a universal service; nevertheless this part of the economy is not allowed to expand or raise its standards, therefore it cannot compete economically or dominate politically.

It is reasonable to speak in this way of a subsistence *minimum* only when there is, in fact, a vast potential surplus, when the minimum can be produced with a small fraction of the social labor and there is opportunity for wide satisfaction at a higher standard. Otherwise one is indirectly flirting with the iron law of wages as a general policy.

Now, as we have suggested, the political execution of

such a divided economy can have the form of a universal
labor service similar to periods of military conscription. Assume conservatively that a tenth of the social labor is required: then a man would serve in the national economy for
six or seven years of his life, spaced out as convenient—
with a certain choice as to the years in which to serve. There
seems to be no reason why a wealthy man could not buy a
substitute to serve his time for him, but this would be at the
prevailing rate of wages in private industry, for why else
should the substitute sell his time? More democratic would
be an arrangement whereby the first period, say 18 to 20,
must be served in person; but later periods, when people
have settled into private affairs, could be served by paid
substitutes. Further details would be the adaptation of different age groups and skills to different kinds of work, the
problems being the same as in any general conscription.

This plan is coercive. In fact, if not in law, however, it is
less coercive than the situation most people are used to.
For the great mass of wage earners, it fixes a limit to the
necessities that, between capital and trade union, they are
subject to; and for the wealthy enterpriser, who would buy
substitutes, it is no more coercive than any other tax. On
constitutional grounds, the crucial objections to forced
labor have always been either that it subjects the individual
to a private enterpriser without contract (a form of slavery);
or it is unfairly competitive; or it broadens the power of the
state. None of these objections holds.

But an important political and economic difficulty of any
such plan is the following: In any divided economy with
double money there are relations between the two economies in which both are directly concerned. On the one hand,
the government can extend its coercion, without the freedom
of the market; this would come up in the exercise of the
right of eminent domain in order to provide the government
with what it must have. On the other hand, the private
economy uses its pressures of monopoly and speculation to
force the government's hand at opportune moments. These

dangers may be mitigated by making the government's business as minimal and as independent of exchange as possible.

Yet in some sphere there *must* be cooperation. These are where the same object is used for minimal and other uses, for instance transportation. For one cannot have two parallel systems of roads, railroads, and airlines. Perhaps, itself moneyless, the government can contribute its share in the form of labor service; and sometimes it can collect credit for its running expenses from the private economy. We are touching on a political principle beyond our scope here, the principle of purity of means in the exercise of the different powers of society. Government, founded on authority, uses mainly the means of personal service; economy, founded on exchange, uses mainly the means of money.

The Standard of Minimum Subsistence

What is the minimum standard on which a person will feel himself secure and free, not struggling to get more in the private economy, unless he chooses? The problem is subtle and difficult, for although as a medical problem it has a definite solution, as a psychological and moral problem it depends on emulation, and who is emulated, and these things themselves are subject to alteration good or bad. What is minimum for even a poor Southern sharecropper might be spendthrifty to an indio of Yucatan (who, however, has other satisfactions).

We are speaking always of a going surplus technology. This technology which can provide all manner of things for everybody can also, in a different way, produce a few things of a very few kinds accompanied by a minimum regulation of time, living arrangements, and habits of life. How seriously are people willing to dispense with many things in order to have the freedom which they also think they want?

When combined with freedom, a minimum standard would be far less than what is estimated minimum in our present society. Let us give a single example. In estimating minimum standards of decency and safety, Stuart Chase finds it indispensable for every home to have a radio, because in an integrated society—especially during a total war —a person must have instant communications (and how desirable to have it one way!). But if the very point of our minimum standard is to free people from "integration," a radio is a convenience which a person might think twice about.

Other examples of reducing the "necessary" minimum could be found by considering how much of decency of appearance and how many contacts are required solely by the fact that we live in a society competitive through and through.

On the other hand, when combined with freedom, our minimum is far higher than exists in a scarcity economy, for instance China, where a person subsists in time-bound service to field or commune (and that standard too, since inevitable, is socially acceptable). But if the very point of our minimum is to free people for a selective choice of how they will regulate their time, mobility and independence of location are indispensable.

The minimum is based on a physiological standard, heightened by the addition of whatever is necessary to give a person a true possible freedom of social choice, and not violating our usual mores.

If freedom is the aim, everything beyond the minimum must be rigorously excluded, even if it should be extremely cheap to provide; for it is more important to limit political intervention than to raise the standard of living.

Then, the minimum economy must produce and distribute:

1. Food sufficient in quantity and kind for health, palatable but without variety.
2. Uniform clothing adequate for all seasons.
3. Shelter on an individual, family, and group basis, with adequate conveniences for different environments.

  4. Medical service.

  5. Transportation.

but *not* primary education which is a public good taxed from the general economy.

Of these, food, clothing, and shelter are produced by absolute mass production in enormous quantities, without variation of style. Medicine and transportation are better provided by some arrangement between the subsistence and general economies.

The Cost of Subsistence

The extent and cost of the proposed subsistence system, measured in current money, is very hard to determine—and therefore it is hard to name, except by guesswork, the number of years of labor service that are bartered away for economic freedom.

In the first place, although the number of laborers is fixed —for even those who would buy off must furnish a laborer as a substitute—the amount of goods to be produced is fluctuating. For, obviously, though all are entitled to the minimal goods, many, and perhaps most, of the people who are used to better and can afford better, will not take them. There is no advantage in taking and wasting, for the less that needs to be produced, the less the exaction of universal service. Different kinds of goods will differ in demand: fewer will use the minimal housing and clothing; most perhaps can use some of the minimum food; very many will use the transportation and medical service. After a sufficient reserve is built up, production is geared to the prospective use of the next year. But further, this demand will fluctuate with the fluctuation of the general economy, though less sharply: in times of general economic crisis, the demand for subsistence goods increases; in times of prosperity, it diminishes. (The fluctuation is less sharp because of the ratio of minimum goods to substitutes of a higher standard, because of the ratio of the number of unemployed to the universal

SUBSISTENCE FRACTION (U.S.)

1932 product created by 35 million people during 70 billion work hours

Assumption: one-half of total production time spent creating capital, luxury, and comfort goods; includes loss by reason of inefficiency and waste

Work hours for production of subsistence in 1932: 35 billion hours

Reduction in hours by reason of technological improvement at 2.5 per cent per year, 1932-44: 24 billion hours required

Production of approximately 25 billion hours of work at rate of 2,500 hours per worker

Reduction of 25 per cent for product not consumed

Labor time reduced to 19 billion hours or 7,600,000 workers

Total labor force equals 80,000,000 workers

Labor force required per annum equals 7,600,000

Therefore:

Required of each worker is that he spend one year of each ten in the labor service

---

(ALL FIGURES IN TERMS OF 1934 PRICES)

Civilian production   War production

1932 — $39 Billion

1939 — $89 Billion

1944 — $88.5 Billion $68.5 Billion

Postwar Goal No. 1 — $135 Billion

Postwar Goal No. 2 — $200 Billion

AN EXCERPT

From an exhaustive list of subsistence goods

(Figures in parentheses indicate amount used per year)

SHELTER EQUIPMENT

Table (1/5)
Chair (1/5)
Cot and mattress (1/5)
Stove—for cooking and heating (1/10)
Fuel (type and quantity dependent on location)
Lamps or other lights (dependent on location)
Pint pot (1/3)
Quart pot (1/3)
12-inch pan (1/3)
Hunting knife, table knife, 2 forks, large and small spoon (1/4)
Corkscrew, can opener (1/4)
Cup, plate, bowl (1/2)
2-gallon pail (1/4)
10-gallon tub for laundry and bathing (1/4)
Mop and broom (1)
Small ax (1/5)
Shovel (1/5)
Household repair kit—hammer, nails, screw driver, etc. (1/2)
10 yards of clothesline, 1 dozen clothespins (1/2)
Dish towels (4)
Cleaning cloths (4 yds.)
Pencils (10)
Writing paper (1 rm.)
Matches (12 boxes of 400)
Flashlight (1/2)
Batteries for flashlight (4)
Kitchen and grease-solvent soaps (25 cakes)

HOW MUCH WOULD THESE THINGS COST UNDER CONDITIONS OF ABSOLUTE MASS PRODUCTION WITHOUT STYLING, FLUCTUATION, PROFITS, MERCHANDISING, ETC.?

Conclusion:

To produce the standard of 1932—well above subsistence as here defined — would require

$$\frac{39}{157} \text{ or } \frac{39}{200}$$

or one year of work in four or five

labor service, and because the reserve functions as an ever-normal granary.)

But secondly, and most importantly, the price of goods under such a system of absolute mass production is impossible to estimate. It would be unbelievably cheap. For clothing, a possible estimate could be gotten from army uniforms, but these are of course produced for profit all along the line; a better figure would be given by the English utility clothing of World War II, which was remarkably cheap compared to the free market. The figure for farm produce is especially difficult: given a system of extensive agriculture like the Soviet state farms, with the problem of distribution simplified by processing on the spot into non-perishable and dehydrated forms, the cost would fall to very little; yet this might not be the most absolutely efficient procedure. Prefabrication in housing has simply not been tried on a large scale; yet small attempts—e.g., TVA 3-rooms-and-bath at $1,900 (1934)—show astounding reductions in price. It would be only for medical service and transportation that one could make reasonable estimates. The rest is guesswork.

Then we guess that to produce subsistence for all Americans would require not more than one-seventh of the available labor time (normal working day) and money. This guess is as of 1945. In 1959 we would guess one-tenth.

Architecture of the Production Centers

In the subsistence economy, there is the architecture of the production centers and of the minimum housing.

The centers are factories and housing for basic manufac-

Some ways of guessing the fraction of the economy needed to provide subsistence. But productivity is increasing at an astonishing rate: for 12-year period 1945–57, rate was 3.3% per year, compared to 2.4% annually for the past 60 years. (Nat. Bur. of Economic Research)

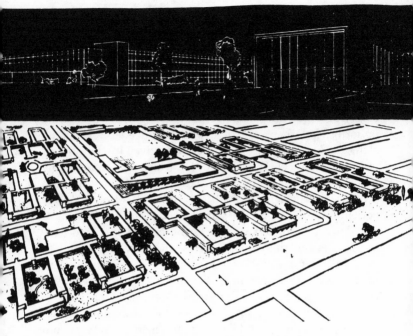

A production center for 5000 workers, within a city

tures, clothing, prefabricated houses, processing of foods; and for industrial farms and fisheries, and such mines as it is wise to run separately rather than jointly with the general economy.

The single principle of these centers of labor service is efficiency. The purely functional approach described in the Soviet functionalist plans (p. 71 and p. 72) is sufficient. If there are idle convertible plants, they would be used. If the centers are located in isolated parts, more elaborate social centers must be provided; but if they are near cities, that is not necessary. Efficiency and cheapness are the only determinants.

Since the quantity of production of certain items may vary from year to year, such plants may be designed to run on two shifts or three shifts. Ordinarily everything runs on maximum capacity.

Centers should be decentralized to the point of maximum efficiency of distribution. The location of industrial farms depends on soil and climate.

Provision is here being made for several million workers —perhaps as many as 12 million. But in the depths of the great Depression there were that many unemployed; and during the war, provision was made for 10 million in the services, luxuriously equipped, without catastrophic dislocation.

A production center for 50,000 workers: 1. Airport 2. Heavy manufacture 3. Light manufacture 4. Industrialized agriculture 5. Housing 6. Sports and social center

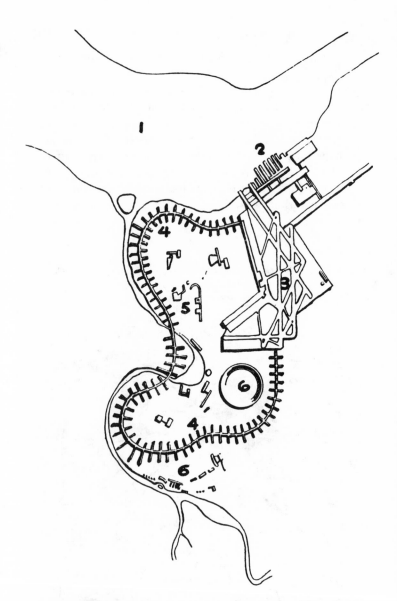

A production center for 75,000 workers in an isolated place:
1. Harbor 2. Docks 3. Airport and factory 4. Housing 5. Com-
munity buildings 6. Sports

Minimum Housing

The housing to be produced falls into several classes. The over-all principles are: (1) Good functioning at a minimum standard; (2) Considerable mobility, combined with exchangeability, to allow freedom of location; (3) Mass production of the fewest possible types *consistent with freedom of selection* on crucial basic issues; (4) Longevity of 10 to 20 years; (5) Adaptation of the types to various communal environments, e.g., those in which public utilities are available, those where they are not available, etc.

The trailers are a restudy of similar houses found practical by the TVA. Another type is the Geodesic structure of Fuller. A third is air inflated. There are other possibilities. One class is adapted to a complete absence of public utilities, therefore has kerosene light, septic tank, etc. These are superior to the actual housing of millions of farm families and they could be used by city families on vacation. Another class is adapted to trailer camps equipped with government utilities, electricity, running water, community kitchens. A somewhat similar community framework for migratory farm workers with tents has been analyzed by the Farm Security Administration. By good planning, larger houses for families can be combined from the units to which members are entitled as individuals.

The plot of land on which the trailer or house is located presents little problem where there are no public utilities, where the population is sparse, and the value of the land submarginal. The difficulty increases where utilities, population, and value increase; up to the point of metropolitan concentration, where the problem is insuperable.

This means that, quite apart from public or private ownership of land, to live in one place rather than another involves a fundamental difference in living standards. This is one of the choices put up to the individual, whether or not he will work for the extra money to pay (in the general economy) the increment above the minimum.

Shelter in a small town

Shelter in the woods

This is an extremely interesting question; viewing the matter from the point of view of our problem, we learn a good deal about urban life. *Metropolitan living, even under slum conditions, is in the class of luxuries.* This is the converse to the well-known proposition that metropolitan living, even on Park Avenue, often has physiologically and sociologically the standard of a slum. (By "metropolis" we mean places over a million; urban environments up to several hundred thousand need not present these difficulties for subsistence housing.)

If we break down the elements of metropolitan rent, we see the causes. First is the extraordinary multiplication of city services—pavements, street lighting and cleaning, water, sewage, etc., biologically necessary because of the concentration, sociologically necessary for policing, etc. Then there are items like parks and museums, ranging from psychological necessity to cultural convenience. These appear as city taxes. Again, the value of land intensively occupied and intensively used by juxtaposition, as by the number of persons passing a particular spot per hour. And the fact that land scarcity is of the essence of concentration, and therefore land is preempted as a business. These factors appear as interest on investment and payment for risk. And then there is the cost of building, which cannot be mass produced because it is sporadic and has peculiar conditions; this appears as wages and profit.

We must conclude that minimal subsistence as such jibes with decentralization but not with metropolitan concentration.

The houses can be pitched only on the outskirts of cities—as in Swedish plans for subsistence housing. In places of a hundred thousand, this is perfectly adequate; but in metropolises it is precisely not being a member of the community. On the other hand, housing of a metropolitan type cannot be provided at a minimal standard. Public housing, heavily subsidized and built on condemned land, still rents at a figure that eats up a fifth or a quarter of a man's income in the general economy.

The metropolis exists by the intricacy of its social inter-dependencies, and it is to maintain these that each one must sacrifice his time and wealth.

What is likely, however, is that one result of the sub-sistence system would be a shortage of common labor in the metropolises, and therefore the employers would have to make efforts to attract such labor.

Away from these big cities, however, millions would live in mobile and exchangeable units, making use of scattered stations. And they would certainly desire, just set free from social necessity, not to settle down to a new job for a time, but to entertain themselves on the free goods of travel, to see like Ulysses, "the places and many minds of men." These are the elements of a radically new kind of com-munity, fluid rather than fixed. Such a profound difference would involve other profound changes, for instance in law.

Mon Repos

A minimal economy settlement: 1. Shelter 2. Mess hall, kitchen and wash house

Teacher! Today Again
Do We Have to Do What We Want to Do?

Now supposing such a system of assured subsistence with almost complete freedom of economic ties were put into effect. No doubt for millions of people, no matter how much they might resist the idea in prospect, the first effect would be immense relief, relief from responsibility, from the pressure of the daily grind, from the anxiety of failure.

But after this first commonplace effect had worn off, the moral attitude of a people like the Americans would be profoundly deranged. They would be afraid not only of freedom and leisure, which release both creative and destructive drives nicely repressed by routine, but especially of boredom, for they would find, or imagine, themselves quite without cultural or creative resources. For in our times all entertainments and even the personal excitement of romance seem to be bound up with having ready money to spend. Emotional satisfaction, too, has been intricated into the motion of the entire productive machine, it is bound up with the Standard of Living. Movies cost money, bars cost money, and having a date costs money. Certainly a car costs money. Apart from these, as everybody knows, there is nothing to do but hang around. (Sports do not cost money, sex does not cost money, art does not cost money, nature does not cost money, intercourse with people does not cost money, science and God do not cost money.)

The Americans would suddenly find themselves "rescued" from the physical necessity and social pressure which alone, perhaps, had been driving them to their habitual satisfactions. They might soon come to regard commercial pleasures as flat and unpalatable, but they would not suddenly thereby find any others. They would be like the little girl in the progressive school, longing for the security of having her decisions made by the grown-ups, who asks, "Teacher, today again do we have to do what we want to do?"

Would it be a salutary boredom to *make* these persons do what they want to do with their time, to discover what they want to do with their lives, rather than following widely advertised suggestions? And not for a couple of weeks of vacation—likewise organized into profit-bearing routines— but year after year. Or would the effect be like the unemployed adolescents on the corner who hang around, apparently unable to think up anything?

We are asking, in the framework of this model proposal, an intensely realistic question about the actual situation in our country. For indeed, in our surplus economy, millions really are technically unemployable—there is no necessary work for them to do, no man's work. If automation were allowed its full headway, these millions would become many many millions. *Because* they are really economically unproductive, they have no culture and no resources of leisure, since culture grows from productive life. At the same time, each one of these people, no matter how he hangs around or perhaps spends his time in getting quasi-visceral "kicks" or being "cool," must also feed his face and come in out of the rain. It is this actuality that our scheme of a divided economy addresses and draws in black and white: we provide the subsistence part in an efficient, honorable, and compulsory way; and we leave open the horrendous question: then what?

The moment when large numbers of people first discover clearly and distinctly that they do not know what they want to do with their time, is fraught with danger. Some no doubt will at once follow any demagogic or fanatical leader who happens along with a time-consuming and speciously thrilling program. (Street-gangs on a mass scale.) How to protect the commonwealth against these bands of bored prejudice? Others, having lost the thread of compulsory mental activity, will wander in the maze of idle idiocy that we associate with degenerate rural classes, except that the food would be even worse, across the counter in a government store.

Jobs, Avocations, and Vocations

The brighter hope is that alongside the leaders teachers would also appear.

The psychoanalysts who deal with the "nervous break-downs" of men of affairs sometimes urge the patient to have the courage to leave his job and embrace his avocation. The job was not freely chosen; it symbolizes and reinforces the very pressures of social and parental authority that have led to disaster. The avocation, presumably, is spontaneous and can draw on deep energy and therefore, by its daily practice, reintegrate the personality.

The system here proposed facilitates such a decision before the stage of modern nervous breakdown. Economically, there would be a recrudescence of small enterprises and the outlay of small venture capital; for the risk of fundamental insecurity of life having been removed, why should not one work to amass a little capital and then risk it in an enterprise that was always sneakingly attractive?

Vocation and "Vocational Guidance"

What now passes for "vocational guidance" and "aptitude testing" is the exact contrary of vocation in the old sense, a man's natural or God-ordained work. The guidance test proceeds from the premise that there is an enormous social-economic machine continually producing society's goods and that this machine must be manned by capable workmen who are cogs in the mechanism. A potential workman is then tested for his physical, emotional, and intellectual aptitudes to find if some part of the man is adapted to performing some role in the machine, most often the role of making a part of a part of a product sold in a distant market.

We have become so accustomed to this picture that it requires a strain of attention to see how simply fantastic it is. The working of the economic society is put first, the life-

work of every individual member of society is not thought of
at all.

In general, a job takes on the nature of a vocation in
the following stages: (a) It satisfies the pressures of a
money-centered society; (b) It is an available means of
making a living; (c) It is personally interesting—has some
relation to friend and family traditions—to childhood ambition; (d) It is a phase of a strong avocation and draws on
free creative energies; (e) It is the kind of experience the
man seeks out. The first, merely economic jobs, are what
most men now have. Family and group jobs were common in
older times. Avocational occupations are a legitimate goal
for society for great numbers of its members; but it demands
more freedom of opportunity and more mature personality
than present circumstances permit. True vocation, however,
is probably not within social means to further (nor even, in
many cases, to prevent).

The Sociological Zoo

A man suddenly withdrawn in will and schedule from
the general economy, and with a lot of time on his hands,
might begin to look at the immense activity of others as at
the objects in a great zoo or museum: a sociological garden
abounding in its tame and savage ways, many of them very
near to humane social behavior and, as monkeys are to men,
all the more curious on that account. This makes a vast
difference in one's joy of life.

Thus, a man may have nothing but pleasant memories of
New York or Paris, even during the summer season. He
speaks of the variety of the city, its easy gait, its shops, parks,
markets and animated streets. And the fact is that he stayed
in these places during the years that he did not have to work
for a living, he was perhaps a student on a scholarship.
Therefore he saw the variety and the out-of-the-way places
that busy people do not stumble on. Projecting his own ease
into the gait of the others, he cannot understand why other

The zoo

critics—for instance, transient visitors who rather project their own hurrying about—judge these people to be nervous or self-centered. Why should not the hot summer be pleasant to a person who can stroll out or not, or go on an excursion? But the rest of the people are hot, indignant, tired, nervous, and bored with their beautiful city, where they are working without much security at tasteless jobs.

To beautify cities, the first step is to change the attitude with which people take their cities.

A small boy, who would reflect the new security of his parents and never feel economic pressure at home, could not fail to find the sociological garden his best school. He would not resent it or distrust it. He would grow up pretty independent, ironical without fierceness, quite amiable, for nothing threatens; a smart-aleck through and through who knows his way around.

The Standard of Living

It would be no small thing for people to understand clearly what poverty consists of—to understand it not in terms of misery or unfortunate cases, but by a universal social standard.

The subsistence standard that we have been describing is, of course, far above that which the majority of the human species in fact subsists on; but it is at least based on physiological, hygienic, climatic, and moral conditions and is not altogether a parochial cultural illusion, fostered by salesmanship, like the Standard of Living of the Americans. The intimate awareness of it would help dispel the attitude of the Americans toward those other peoples as not quite being human beings at all.

CHAPTER 8

Conclusion

These three paradigms are, to repeat it, not plans; they are models for thinking about the possible relations of production and way of life. Let us now say a few words about the relevance of these different modes of thought to different real situations in the world today.

Scheme I

Scheme I is drawn from the tastes and drives of America that are most obvious on the surface—its high production, high Standard of Living and artificially-induced demand, its busy full employment. Much of this is now characterized by our moralists as useless and unstable. There is sharp criticism of the skimping on public goods when the production of frivolous private goods is so unbridled. Even worse, it is pointed out that the superabundance of private goods without the leavening of public goods (education, social services, wiser use of land) is destructive of the satisfactions of even the private goods. It is the aim of Scheme I to answer these complaints, to show how both public *and* private goods in full quantity can cooperate, assuming that we have the productivity for everything, which we have.

To put it another way, our thought is to make a useless economy useful for something great, namely magnificence. The ideal of commercial grandeur is Venice, and we can aspire to it, to assume again the magnificence that human beings wear well. We have to think up some style or other to match the glamour of our coming interplanetary fleets.

More particularly, we as New Yorkers have had in mind

218

our native city, and we have set down some suggestions for the public improvement of New York (Appendices A to D).

Scheme III

Scheme III, for the direct production of subsistence goods, has obvious applications to regions that are poorly industrialized but densely populated. Shaking off colonialism and aspiring to industrialism, these regions have tended to adopt just the opposite policy, to industrialize totally as rapidly as possible and "catch up." The emphasis is on heavy industry, involving unaccustomed hard work now and abstaining from consumers' goods till the future. Also, so far as the Americans have given or lent capital to these regions, we have had no policy and so our tendency is to repeat our own economic pattern.

The policy of heavy industry has great disadvantages. It involves stringent dictatorship to plan huge goals and to enforce completely new work habits. There are no skills. It involves the breaking-up of age-old community forms with almost certain moral and youth problems coming in the wake. It guarantees much over-investment in disastrous mistakes, with waste of wealth and human suffering.

Just the opposite policy makes more sense: to start off by using the most advanced techniques to provide universal subsistence, and for the rich countries to give or lend the capital specific for this purpose. People are at once better off; they have more time. They then have the freedom to make their own community adjustments. Political pressure is low and state regulation is minimized. In the production of subsistence goods, there cannot be great mistakes, nothing is totally wasted. But further, the plan has the advantage of rapidly generating a more complicated economy and heavy industry *under its own steam*. For when people have once been raised above utter misery and given a tolerable security, they begin to have other wants and have the spirit and energy and a little money to try and satisfy them. Also, having used the machines for subsistence, they now have skills and work-habits. It is at this point that the production and import of other capital goods will come by popular demand, in the people's own style. Finally, such a plan would involve less suffering.

But in advanced countries too this scheme is not irrelevant. (Something like it, we think, was first proposed in the Weimar Republic.) For surplus productivity can lead to widespread unemployment as a *desirable* possibility; and this is a simple, honorable, and stabilizing way of coping with the problem.

Scheme II

Being artists, the authors of this book are naturally partial to the middle mode of thinking, Scheme II, where the producing and the product are of a piece and every part of life has value in itself as both means and end; where there is a community tradition of style that allows for great and refined work, and each man has a chance to enhance the community style and transform it.

Such a commune is utopian, it is in the child-heart of man, and therefore it is easiest to think of it as growing in virgin territory with new people.

If we think of the underdeveloped regions that are sparsely settled and rich in resources, parts of Siberia, Alaska or Africa, the Columbia River Basin or parts of South America, self-sufficient regionalism on a quality standard makes sense. Such regions could be most harmoniously developed not by importing into them the total pattern of advanced technology (as is being done), but by the kind of industrial-agricultural symbiosis we have described, drawing always on their own resources and working them up themselves. If the old total pattern is simply reproduced in the new place, the first stage of a virgin area will be a colonial dependency, exporting raw materials; the final stage will be a merging into the national whole with no new cultural contribution. But we need the new contribution. On the other hand, the quicker and more harmoniously the new place achieves a regional self-sufficiency, the more independently and selectively it can cope with the complex national culture on its own terms, and the more characteristic its own contribution can be. A fresh region represents nature full of the possibilities of invention; an established economy is necessarily in the strait jacket of bad habits.

Scheme IV: A Substitute for Everything

There is, of course, still a fourth attitude toward the economy of abundance that is socially viable and implies a fourth community scheme. This is to put the surplus into combustibles and, igniting these, to destroy a more or less (it is hard to be sure) regulated part of the production and consumption goods, and the producers and the consumers. Recent studies in this mode of thinking have hit on techniques for the dislocation of industry into mountain-fastnesses, the non-illumination of streets, the quickest way to hasten to the most deadly spot, the esthetics of invisibility, the enlivening of the atmosphere with radioactivity, and, in general, an efficient schedule for returning from the Sixth to before the First Day.

The Need for Philosophy

Mostly, however, the thousand places that one plans for have mixed conditions and mixed values. The site and history of a place are always particular, and these make the beauty of a plan. Different people in a place want different things, and the same people want different things. Some of these conditions and aims are compatible and some are incompatible—the musician, says Plato, knows which tones will combine and which will not combine. It's a difficult art that we have to learn. Other nations have had long experience in developing their cities and villages. We can learn a

"INITIATION, EDUCATION, GOVERNMENT
these are three synonymous words"
                                    MICHELET

lot from them, but we cannot learn the essential things, how to cope with the modern plight.

For in the present period of history, we Americans are the oldest and most experienced people in the world. We were the first to have the modern political revolution and the maturity of the industrial revolution. These, combined with our fortunate natural resources and geography, have made us the first to experience the full impact of the high Standard of Living and a productivity that improves, technically, nearly 4% a year. As the first to experience it, we are deeply disappointed in progress, confused, afraid of serious decisions, and therefore reactionary and conformist in important matters. Yet as the oldest and most experienced, we have the responsibility to be wise.

One way or another, there is no doubt that the Americans are going to be spending a lot more on public goods. The so-called Urban Renewal program is at present important and will be more so. It is essential that these new efforts make sense, not only to avoid misusing the money but because it is the nature of a physical plant that once built it stays and stays. Ignorant and philistine planning long ago saddled us with many of our present problems. It continues to do so. Ameliorative plans are then proposed—a new subway, a new highway, slum-clearance—which soon reproduce the evil in a worse degree. We then have the familiar proliferation of means, of feats of engineering and architecture, public goods, when what is needed is human scale. People are rightly suspicious of planning, and they end up with everything being overplanned, no freedom from the plan, and the purpose lost. This is because nobody has dared to be philosophical, to raise the question of the end in view, rather than merely trying to get out of a box.

It is understood by sociologists, anthropologists, and psychologists that the different functions of men and groups cohere in whole patterns of culture. But our physical planning in the most sensitive areas, like housing or schools, is carried on with eyes shut to the whole pattern. For instance, housing is discussed in terms of bio-sociological standards of decency and cost problems of land and construction, but not much attention is paid to the kind of community resulting. The community has increasing class stratification and increasing juvenile delinquency, effects that were not aimed at. But of course, to avoid pressing community problems and to concentrate on "practical" solutions—and to exclude minorities and increase delinquency—*is* now the pattern of our culture. Is this inevitable?

Bosanquet said somewhere that the characteristic of philosophy is to be concrete and central. By concrete and central he would mean, in our present subject, directly attending to the human beings, the citizens of the city, their concrete behavior and their indispensable concerns, rather than getting lost in traffic problems, housing problems, tax problems, and problems of law enforcement. It is concrete to plan work, residence, and transit as one problem. It is

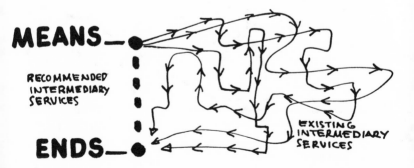

central to keep one's eyes on the center of the target, the community and its way of life, not exaggerating production, the Standard of Living, or special interests out of all pro-portion.

In this difficult art, the people are not philosophical, they do not know the concrete and central facts. Yet only the people *can* know them. The answer is in the remarkable and thought-provoking sentence of Michelet: "Initiation, education, and government—these are three synonomous words."

Afterword: Communitas revisited

Percival Goodman

My brother had said no when I outlined my version of a book I proposed to call *Communitas Revisited*. I had thought that, after so many years, we could collaborate again in second guessing the future. But he said that he had no time and that he no longer believed in schemes for improving the human condition.

It was true. In his last years, Paul had lost confidence in our species and he didn't, in fact, have time. He died two months later.

So I was faced with a task that I thought must be done in order to correct an important oversight in *Communitas*. The result was *The Double E*, linking Ecology and Economy. This afterword is taken from that part of the book which deals not with the problems of the present, but with a possible, brighter future. The paradigm is based on my belief that people are life-oriented, rather than death-oriented, and will not, except by mischance, destroy the earth and themselves.

Let me admit that, when I developed this fourth paradigm about a decade ago, my optimism, then as now, was based on shaky grounds. But, without hope, what do we have?

When Paul and I wrote *Communitas*, it was, we presumed, feasible to recommend many possibilities since "for the first time in history, spectacularly, we have in the United States, a surplus technology, a technology of free choice that allows for the most widely various community arrangements and ways of life."

The presumption was correct, but who could have guessed how quickly our appetites would grow, how quickly our surplus would diminish, and how badly we would choose?

Almost a half-century later what had seemed an everbrimming cornucopia threatens to run dry. Limits, not free choice, scarcity, not surplus, are now the facts that will condition our future. Depletion of the ozone layer above, industrial and atomic pollution on and under our earth, oil shortages in the U.S, are among the problems of which we are aware.

Times of change are hard for planners as well as for prophets. Prediction becomes guesswork, and the most solidly based research may lead to absurd conclusions. Nevertheless, the planner cannot be fainthearted. He must have the courage to interpret what he sees in the light of his own vision and have the daring to make assumptions even when they are contrary to the wisdom of his peers and of the past.

What has happened is not only technical, it is total; and so drastic as to suggest mutation rather than evolution. We live in a world of improbabilities come true—a world not so solid, earthy, and dependable as we thought, a world suddenly seen as a fragile network of interlocking, interdependent systems in imminent danger of overburden and disruption.

In such a time it would be expected that such words as "ecology" and "economy" would haunt all discussions of planning. Not so. Architects and planners, like businessmen and even statesmen, are fixated on a science and technology, an ideology and an economics closer to 1900 than 2000. With few exceptions, they seem incapable of realizing that there has been a change in quantity—like the ultimate straw breaking the camel's back—making the qualitative change to which we must address ourselves.

"Ecology" and "economy" are two powerful words linked by the Greek *oikos*, meaning house. The root meaning of *ecology* is a knowledge of the house; *economy* means management of the house. Modern usage doubles the impact: *ecology* being the study of mutual relations between organism and environment, *economy* the management of expenditures. Are not these the operative concepts in planning for a world with diminishing resources and increasing populations?

The Built Environment

Like a poem, the built environment has always been more than the sum of its parts, but unlike a poem—which may be achieved by an individual out of his own psyche—it is a collective work calling for many skills, using solid chunks of the planet in its making and subtly or overtly conditioning our movements. Throughout history these sticks and stones have been a crystallization of the technical, social, and moral qualities of the society that did the building, a crystallization of its way of life showing how it spent its substance, what it revered, admired, loved, and cherished as well as to what it paid no heed.

The built environment of the late twentieth century differs from the past not merely because it uses greater chunks of material to make it, not merely because everything is more complicated and needs more fuel to keep it going, but because it no longer evolves from the climate, geography, or history of the place where it is, nor is it the collective work of the people who inhabit it; instead, the new environment is conceived at conference tables and pieced together on drawing boards, its design aspiring to be the result of computerized decision-making suitable to the printed circuits of a society transformed into technology.

During most of the twentieth century the future has been projected as just such an artificial, urbanized world in which human muscle long ago replaced by machine is now preparing the next stage—the human brain replaced by machine, the human brain redundant. The world is conceived as a colony of vast termitaries run by agencies, conglomerates, and cartels who are in turn directed by a queen computer buried in the air-conditioned depths.

How fortunate it is that such a simple fact as the need to live within our means precludes such a future and rids us of all those boring discussions on the moral and social implications of life in such a world.

We know now at what a disquieting rate the machines have been using up mines, oil deposits, and forests; how much they pollute in the course of their producing and what they produce is also a pollutant. Quite suddenly we've come to realize what mismanagement and ignorance of nature's symbiotic ways have done or threatens to do to our planet.

Few nowadays think it cranky to say that there is an immediate cause for worry not only as to the quality of life on earth but even as to its continuance. Nevertheless, I realize that when I conclude there can be no acceptable future, perhaps no future at all, without the dismantling of the war machine, population control by humane means, and a curbing of appetites by democratic process, I go further than many.

A viable future assumes users inclined toward modesty and a certain frugality, who favor a physical environment designed for people, not things, and who will support plans based on the scale of humankind in its symbiotic relationship with nature.

Based on these values, I had tried to project a future society by answering the following questions: What are the ways of creating more feasible man-made environments? What are the form-making elements and how should we use them? In a general way, what would the routine of daily life be like in such a future habitat and what would it look like?

Assumptions and Predictions

Here is a fourth model based on the same aesthetic and ethical standards used in the three previous models, but with premises that reflect additional concerns. Here there are crude physical restraints; scarcity not surplus, not a cornucopia but a small planet with burgeoning populations and diminishing resources. Here I accept the need to control technology since we will soon be unable to cope with some of its by-products (unemployment, pollution) nor afford some of its products (gadgetry, death-dealing machines). Here I assume that certain trends in our culture will become dominant modes—among them a more communal way of life, sexual equality, an altogether simpler standard of living, a decentralization of work and political processes. . . .

This fourth paradigm too is embodied in a physical model, for this form seems now (as it did then) the best way for an architect to present a proposal. However, a model of this sort is an abstraction from and a simplification of the real world. It is therefore *not* a model in the sense of an architectural model, as the focus is not on the concrete form but the form-making elements, be they ethical, social, technical, economic, or aesthetic. The purpose of the model is predictive: to sketch a probable future if certain alternatives are selected. I have tried to select alternatives that I assume may find acceptance because the others (in my estimation) range from the improbable to the disastrous.

The basic assumption of the fourth paradigm is that we all seek life, liberty, and the pursuit of happiness and it is a possible goal.

I also assume those demographers right who forecast that during the early decades of the twenty-first century the world's population will have at least doubled before a leveling off in growth occurs.

A third assumption is that we have reached a plateau in technological change in all branches except the life sciences.

Finally I predict that by the year 2020, the nations will meet, vote for life, not for death, and that universal disarmament will follow.

The Year 2020

Planning

During the last stages of Western industrial society, the exploitation of land, transportation modes, and engineering design dominated physical planning theory. Now, the aim of architects and physical planners is to relate spaces and structures so their arrangement facilitates a convivial rapport between domestic life and work, education and leisure, privacy and community, expressing through their forms an aesthetic vision which makes sense of it all.

In addition, there is another: the requirement to accommodate the needs of the world-wide organization that came to be called the Basic Economy predicated on the relationship between ecology and economy, and the need for recognizing both concepts.

The Fourth Paradigm

As the nations began to disarm, it was agreed that the vast stores of skills and resources now free would be used to implement the basic requirement for world peace: *All people must have elementary subsistence as a right.*

The first step was to agree that the right to participate in the society and earn freedom from want is the birthright of all. The Basic Economy was organized to implement this right.

The principles of the Basic Economy are few: A fraction of the world's production is taken out of the economy of all nations in proportion to their wealth. This fraction consists of the goods required for a minimum but healthful subsistence for all. There is no variation in quality or quantity because of higher or lower standards of living as the goods are *not* for comfort or luxury, but *subsistence.*

The rest was logistics. How can the deprived of all nations be fed, clothed, and housed in the most efficient way? How can all people be insured against want? How can these things be done with minimum damage to global resources, minimum infringement on human freedom? The answers were set forth in a law called *World Conservation of Natural (including Human) Resources.* The premises on which the law is based are simple to the point of banality: "Planetary resources are finite and must be conserved; planetary life depends on maintaining

a balance between organism and environment; earth is an oa-
sis of life in space, the human race is probably unique, a species worth preserving."

It was recommended that the rich nations provide the poor
with the means to mass-produce subsistence goods and teach
them how to use and maintain the machinery and technology.
With survival assured, with the energy given by an adequate
diet, suitable shelter, and proper medical care, with the
learning of modern skills and work habits, the people would
soon be able to decide on life styles compatible with both
their ways and the new technology.

Organization of the Basic Economy

An international committee monitors the Basic Economy
organization set up by each nation. Each nation provides the
co-operating force through a universal draft.

Although the function of the Basic Economy is to provide
subsistence goods in the most efficient way, the well-being of
the producers takes precedence. The schedule of work is designed to avoid long periods of routine and mechanical work
with opportunity provided and time allowed for other activities; the cooperators urged to do their service in foreign parts
learn new languages, develop new skills and new interests, all
with the aim of making the work period a broadening, stim-
ulating, and democratizing experience.

The disbanded military plant, its lands and equipment, are
converted to create the initial production centers of the Basic
Economy. Thus the ancient prophecy is fulfilled: The swords
are beaten into plowshares and the spears into pruning hooks.

Style

Broadly speaking, the goods now produced fall into three
categories:

First, *the machine style,* symbolized by the ball bearing
whose function requires that each be exactly like the next in

its series—of equal sphericity, density, polish, etc.—and there be many of them. Machine-style goods, impersonal, standardized, mass-produced, are shaped for absolute efficiency and minimum use of materials compatible with performance.

This is the style of pure utility, the style of the Basic Economy, of bridges and dams, of airplanes, computers, saws, hammers, and all other tools.

Second, the symbol for *hand-style goods* could be a sculpture or a painting. The object is personal, the whim of the maker may be a sufficient excuse for its being, and it need not appeal to everyone; it may, in fact, only appeal to the maker and need have no function except to be itself.

The mode of production of the third style is *intermediate*, for it combines many of the tools and techniques of the machine style with much of the personal quality of the hand style. There is no search for maximum efficiency and utility as no large numbers of like objects are to be made, complete accuracy and uniformity are not desiderata. As an example of this mode consider the making of chairs: Chairs for an auditorium seating a thousand should be made by machine, but chairs in one's living room? A man with leisure and a knack for this kind of thing feels it is worthwhile to make a chair as a singular and expressive act.

These styles are not mutually exclusive; to the contrary, it is just in their interaction that the form-making potential is best expressed. So with other things: clothes, housewares, and all personal objects. Here, then, we have the handicraft movement dreamed of by Ruskin and Morris, but no longer a dream since it is based on the freed time given by our advanced technology.

Centralization, Decentralization

As a principle in twenty-first-century organization, decentralization is the preferred way, as its opposite tends to go out of scale, is always politically risky, often technologically unnecessary, and generally economically inefficient. However, the several styles of production have helped to focus on the vexing question of what should be centralized, dispersed, or decentralized. Surely there would be great difficulty in attempting to centrally plan or produce hand- or intermediate-style goods. Machine-style goods, on the other hand, being designed for simple utility, mass-produced, and having a high degree of efficiency as the major criterion, may require concentrating authority, large-scale planning, tight scheduling.

Similarly, in locating and designing routes, whether for trains or planes, water or electrical power, in controlling pollution or preventing epidemics, allocating or replenishing natural resources and the like, centralization of authority and comprehensive planning are essential.

Reform of Work

By the middle of the twentieth century the scientific and technical management teams in the industrially advanced countries had developed systems capable of producing all needed goods and services, but ultimately two facts became clear: Fully automated processes were theoretically possible but not as practical as people plus machines, since automated machines could make goods but not buy them, a bad thing for the economy; and they deprived people of a major psychological need—useful work, a bad thing for the society.

By the end of the twentieth century, three general principles emerged as basic to postindustrial production:

First, a program of work designed on psychological and social as well as technological considerations. The program provides for diversified employment designed to aid in the development of sane and healthy people, as well as to produce goods.

Second, consultation with all experienced workers in the design of the products, the machines that make them, and the plants in which they are housed.

And third, participation by all workers in management. (The most important question is still unresolved: *Who shall decide on what is to be made?* Workers, management, the market, or some social, ethical, or political principle?)

A major change in production techniques is seen in the increase in small-sized shops making intermediate-style goods as well as parts for machine-style goods. This plus the reforms in the work process based on worker participation and more flexible scheduling, has again made it possible to relate the means of livelihood to the way of life. Home and workshop, often combined in the same building or neighborhood, are now a lively force in educating the young, forming communal ties, fostering creative work, and developing pride of place.

Economy of Services

By the last third of the twentieth century a person in the technologically advanced West consumed ten times more energy and polluted his environment many times more heavily than his counterpart in the Third World, a result in no small part of the fabrication and use of harebrained elaborations which had become the major product of the perverse technology.

A whole branch of twenty-first-century technology is devoted to rediscovering or inventing simple ways to use natural forces in a nonpolluting way—capturing solar heat or wind force, using the rise and fall of tides, the evaporation of water, the harnessing of volcanoes, as well as the more mundane conversion of waste materials.

"Why plant dead posts in the ground and wait for them to rot? Why not plant live trees instead and let them bear fruits and nuts?" (Philadelphia Agricultural Society, 1819).

Living Arrangements

Compartmentalization, specialization, and mechanical scheduling were characteristic of the twentieth-century living: Work was quarantined from other affairs, domestic life had its compartment, as did play; the young were kept separate from the old, family from family, sex from sex, means from ends. Theory and practice rarely mixed. Though there was much talk of democracy, segregation of people by color and/or income was common. Maps by planners looked like kindergarten coloring exercises: *commerce* in one color here, *manufacture* there in another. In the residential districts were zones for separate houses on one-acre plots, while in others there might be attached dwellings twelve to the acre, or apartments housing two hundred or even four hundred families on a similar acre.

But change was in the air. Led by the young without an ideology, without organization, a shift toward other living arrangements became apparent during the early 1960s. Camaraderie between the sexes and the discarding of prudery achieved an openness especially marked in the upbringing of children. For the young, it was a rough period, the action sometimes excessive but generally toward simpler and more direct living arrangements, which as time passed became the accepted style for all ages.

By 2020, many schools had become "popular academies in which there is neither pupil nor master, where the people come freely to get free instruction if they need it, and in which they, rich in their own expertise, will teach many things to the professors who in their turn shall bring them the knowledge they lack" (Bakunin). Soon such "popular academies" had become an integral part of all community activity; libraries, restaurants, shops, were all considered environments for learning, as were the ateliers and work places within the town, the factories and farms on the outskirts or in the countryside. It was not as chaotic as it sounds, for then, as now, electronic linkages and the memory banks of computers provided the basis for an orderly curriculum.

Domestic arrangements: The typical institution around which daily activity was organized, the twentieth-century nuclear family, is pretty much a thing of the past, since it was wasteful of resources, vulnerable in time of trouble, and the least friendly form of domestic life conceivable. Households now vary in size and organization. The loner and single-generation blood kin family are found, but the majority of people have opted for family groupings composed of those related by affinity and interest more often than by blood.

The twenty-first-century house plan is in many ways closer to chateaux and manor houses than to those of the last century. A more communal style of living is reflected in the large public rooms and general spaciousness, since living and working accommodations are often needed for households numbering twenty or more people. Some are even larger, such as those organized by the followers of Charles Fourier, who have formed households where a hundred or more families live and work together. This housing designed to accommodate the changing social groupings is gradually replacing these twentieth-century storage units called apartment houses, as well as the detached cottages of suburbia.

The emerging street pattern is also reminiscent of an older time: The town plan is compact as if contained within walls (beyond is the countryside). The streets are narrow by the old motorcar standard, and although there are no uniform replacements and few legal restrictions, the individual houses, as in the streetscapes of medieval towns, relate to each other in a strikingly easy way. This, of course, is not chance but the result of an evolving architectural aesthetic based on a close analysis of function, a straightforward use of appropriate materials, and a respect for the Geddesian triad of "Place, Work, and Folk."

Transportation

Among the generations of man there were centuries of pyramid building, centuries of cathedral building, and a century of automobile building. It is understandable that people would spend their treasure to celebrate kings or gods, but for a people to spend their treasure in celebrating mobility. . . In retrospect it seems unbelievable that both the young and the mature of the twentieth century were seized by this madness which, I have had to conclude, killed more people, wasted more resources, was more polluting, and led to greater migrations of people than the combined wars of that bellicose century. During the height of the automania, a zoologist observed that in animal herds excessive mobility was a sure sign of distress and asked whether this might not be true of his fellow human beings. Perhaps it was distress . . . but what historian can list all the causes that led twentieth-century man to race from highway to byway, tunnel to bridge? Suffice to say that he seemed to be constantly going from where he didn't want to be to where he didn't want to stay.

The folly of automobility is now over. As the new attitude priced unnecessary transportation out of daily life, people discovered the deplorable conditions in which they lived and began to improve them. Now the place where one is tends to be the place where one wants to be; as a consequence almost three quarters of the rubber-tired vehicles have disappeared. The savings in petroleum alone were immense. More important was the effect on health. Eliminating the pollution caused by these vehicles, and the generally slower pace (once people got accustomed to it), are credited with a marked reduction in the incidence of respiratory and stress diseases. And of course there are few traffic accidents.

The twenty-first century has the problem of dismantling over half of the most elaborate, extensive, and costly structures ever built by man, the infrastructure on which the automobile depended: garages and service stations, roads and highways, tunnels, bridges, and viaducts. Those routes that remain in use have had their magnificent engineering finally tested— they are reserved for high-speed traffic only.

Although there is a great deal less movement of people and goods than was common during the latter part of the twentieth century, traffic still is substantial. Bus, truck, rail, and waterway systems have been reorganized and operate as integrated and flexible networks.

A major shift has occurred in overland air transport. Most standard fixed-wing planes of the twentieth century have been rejected in spite of their superb design, since the noise pollution along the rising and descending flight paths was unacceptable, as was the inordinate amount of land required for airport runways. The obvious solution was to improve the helicopter and the vertical take-off and landing (VTOL) planes.

For short daily trips, skates, bicycles, and a variety of tricycles are common, along with the small slow-speed buses which crisscross the towns, and though railroad trackage is much used for long-haul transportation, high-speed buses and trucks run between towns and serve less densely settled areas.

Land Use

Twentieth-century economics held that insofar as each unit of land is different from another and the differences have economic significance, unequal demand is created so land costs will differ. Such considerations led to intense use of land having the highest cost often regardless of the consequences. The current restraints imposed now prevent such abuses. As an instance, undesirably high densities are made unpractical, since in present practice the conservation laws restrict the use of elevators and moving stairways to buildings of special purpose, thus the height of buildings is restricted to the stair-climbing ability of the inhabitants. It is not zoning laws that restrict a building's location of ground coverage but the requirement that it be made comfortable by maximum dependence on the ancient means—sun and shade, exposure to breeze, protection against the gale.

Like the elevator, mechanical ventilation and air conditioning are reserved for special situations—operating rooms, laboratories, concert halls, tunnels, and submarines. A building technology dependent on gadgetry belongs to the past since it was wasteful, catered to the architects' laziness, and threatened to fill the world with identically shaped boxes or, worse, buildings shaped by ego.

With most travel by foot, bike, or short-haul bus, common sense dictates a close relationship between work and living places, and since all is designed for the convenience of people moving under their own steam, recreation space and the countryside are near. The planner, instead of basing his layouts on the circulation of bulky vehicles and their storage, bases himself on the movement of people passing through pleasant places. That romantic Viennese Camille Sitte is in style, and John Ruskin is quoted: "The first school of beauty must be the streets of your city. . . ."

As in all good plans, convenience and delight merge. Nature's variety and man's skill are seen at the eye level and pace of the pedestrian, not through the windshield at sixty miles an hour as in automania days. A sudden rise, a river's edge, the prevailing breeze, the arc of the sun, all enter into the calculations of the urban designer establishing street directions, landmarks, and boundaries, the juxtaposition of built and open spaces, the siting of buildings. . . .

Metamorphosis of Metropolis

Huge cities had become progressively less habitable and lost the larger part of their population. Unsafe to live in, uneconomic to manage, they had become, through the inept decisions of central governments, the last resort of the poorest and least urbanized people.

As the physical pattern changed, so did the pattern of government. The municipal agencies, overstaffed, overpaid, and underproductive, which had monopolized all city services and brought the city to bankruptcy were disbanded, and in their place were developed neighborhood-government units which had the authority to purchase services from other units, from private concerns, or from their own personnel. The world-famous fantasy known as Manhattan Skyline no longer symbolizes a citadel of business but a museum city, a tourist attraction like Venice or Paris Centre.

New Town Theory

The Industrial Revolution created and developed the metropolis, its aftermath destroyed it. During this latter period, then called the "crisis of our cities," innumerable theories were propounded and plans drawn, ranging from the plodding efforts of bureaucratic Gradgrinds to the fantasies of genius, all showing ways of altering the old to fit the changing conditions or proving that the sole solution is to start afresh with startling ideas.

Looking back it is a surprise to find that it was not a Le Corbusier, a Kenzo Tange, nor even a Frank Lloyd Wright who forecast the principles of postindustrial town planning, but a Victorian, John Ruskin writing in *Sesame and Lilies* in the lush prose for which he and his period were known:

> Through sanitary and remedial action in the houses that we have; and then the building of more, strongly, beautifully, and in groups of limited extent, kept in proportion to their streams and walled around, so that there be no festering and wretched suburb anywhere, but clean and busy streets within and open country without, with a belt of beautiful garden and orchard around the walls, so that from any part of the city perfectly fresh air and grass and sight of far horizon might be reachable in a few minutes walk. This is the final aim.

Was the aim a pre-Raphaelite vision of a medieval town Ebenezer Howard's Garden City, or the Goodmans' New Commune moved into a new century? Surely none of these, yet in every period there are works that forecast what is to come.

A Populated Area

In this paradigm our first diagram called "The Zones" shows the development of a town and its environs. It consists of a compactly built up center, a ring of gardens, another of larger farms, and, beyond, open country.

The zones: (1) town, (2) kitchen gardens, (3) large-sized farms, (4) Basic Economy food production center, (5) grazing, open country, (a) highway and railroad, (b) along ring road: farms, power plants, food processing, Basic Economy camps, (c) airport, (d) outdoor sports areas at corners of town.

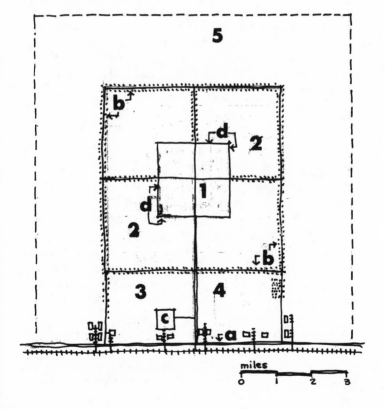

miles
0   1   2   3

The built-up part of the town, four square miles in area, houses the activities of 128,000 people at an average density of 50 to the acre. So disposed as to be less than a mile away from anyone in the town are the sport fields and courts, swimming places and picnic grounds. An acre of garden space is allotted to every 10 inhabitants. These allotments are a mile in width surrounding the town and bordered by a ring road. Along the road are centers (to be described shortly) that service farms and gardens; factories; the borders of large farms; and the Basic Economy settlements.

Some five miles from the town center is the main highway and railroad, reached by the ring road and a road leading directly into town. Between town and highway are large, mechanized farms and a Basic Economy food production center. Dispersed along the main transportation routes are the large-sized factories, refineries, and the like, as well as the VTOL-port. Around this entire complex of uses is the green belt, as nearly untouched nature as man can abide.

Town

Diagramatically the town is divided into four districts so disposed as to bring the goal of most daily trips within easy walking distance or short bike or bus rides. It is but a five-minute walk to the end of the built-up area from any district center while the ring road is only two miles away. Except for factories incompatible with the living environment and the like, segregation of function is avoided: work places and living places are often the same, eliminating commutation and making most activity part of the intimate, domestic, community scene.

Each of the districts is also divided into four neighborhoods.

The political structure of the town is simple: The neighborhoods elect representatives to the district councils, and the

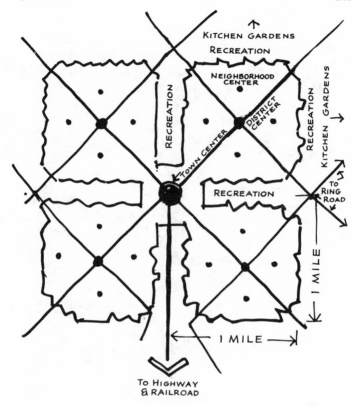

KITCHEN GARDENS

RECREATION

NEIGHBORHOOD CENTER

RECREATION

DISTRICT CENTER

TOWN CENTER

RECREATION

KITCHEN GARDENS

RECREATION

TO RING ROAD

1 MILE

1 MILE

TO HIGHWAY & RAILROAD

Diagram for a town with 128,000 people per 4 square miles. Density: 50 persons to the acre.

district councils appoint the town's officers, who in turn select a chairman.

Out of this diagram emerges a plan sketched to suggest an ambiance of informality, unpretentiousness, and friendly scale where one would hope to find, unexpectedly, some little masterpiece of civic art.

There are a variety of squares and plazas. Here in the

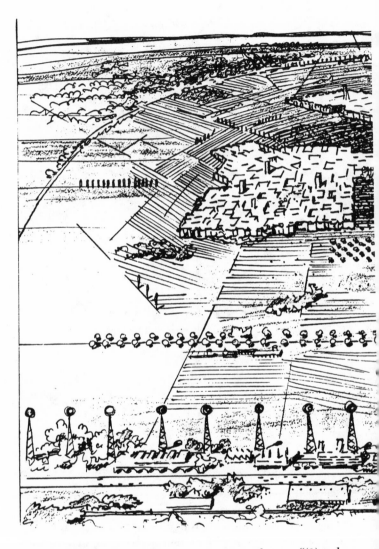

A town plan based on the diagram. The principles are: "(1) to have most functions within walking or bicycling distance, and (2) to have

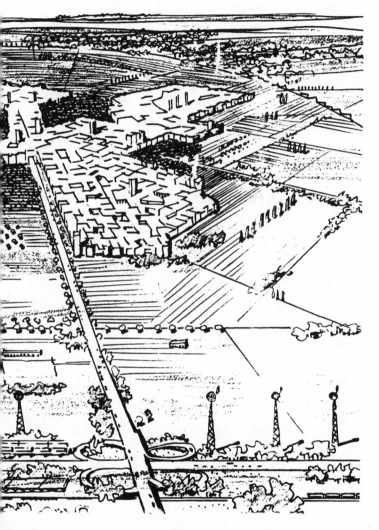

nothing zoned in isolation except nuisance industries." (A) Recreation areas, (B) kitchen gardens, (C) the ring road, (D) farms.

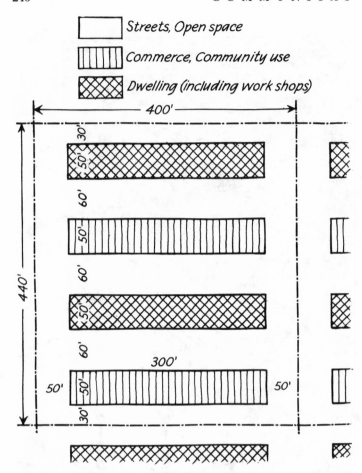

Establishing density in the town. Dwellings: average height 3½ stories.

neighborhoods are found small shops and perhaps some special activity that attracts visitors from other parts; in the districts, seats of local administration, clinics, cafés.

The Town Center is the site of the major shops, the City

Hall, perhaps a museum, a television studio and concert hall, a factory producing some object for which the town is famous. . . .

In general the street pattern is based on a regular module, though varied to take advantage of the topographical conditions as well as provide a variety of streetscapes. The houses front on two streets, one for play and pedestrians, the other for the limited vehicular traffic.

There are four major athletic areas, each with its swimming pools, ponds, playfields, and courts, each convenient to the district it serves.

Leading out from the built area are roads that, as they meander toward the ring road, serve the kitchen gardens. Along some of these roads and paths enterprising gardeners, following Chinese farming practice in the 1970s, have built lineal greenhouses. Others are more direct, connecting city streets to the ring road, since trucking through the town is prohibited. Lining the ring road are small farms and related light industries.

Beyond the ring road are large farms, and the open country.

A street . . . As in preindustrial towns the blocks are short and the street width tends to vary, though few are as broad as those in twentieth-century cities. However, as in medieval towns the intersections often widen into plazas.

. . . *and the houses on it.* A street will usually be lined with three- or four-storied buildings, more often than not containing home and workshop. These houses vary in size but none are as large as those in last century's cities, nor as small as those in the old suburbs. The "grain" of the street (as urban designers used to call it) is closer to Paris before rather than after Haussmann.

Not untypical are the house plans illustrated. *The paired house* (next page, left) is shared by some thirty adults and children in two households. One produces a variety of small parts for an electronics firm while the other designs and makes rather modish women's clothes. The street floor of the house is di-

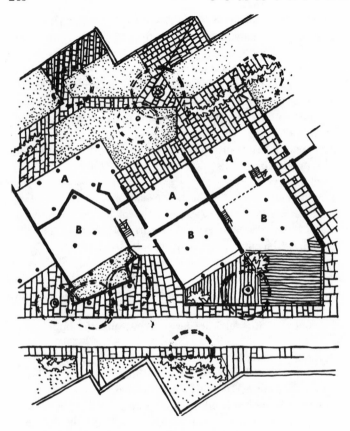

A variety of households. Main floor: (A) kitchen-commons, (B) work-room.

vided between the workshop and the farm-style kitchen-living rooms, a busy and sometimes noisy place whose activities often spill out onto the paved terraces. Above is a double-storied quiet living-library space surrounded by the household's private rooms. The toilet and bath are communal. The roof is a garden on which are often set greenhouses or sheltered areas for sun bathing.

The house on the right is shared by a sculptor and painter,

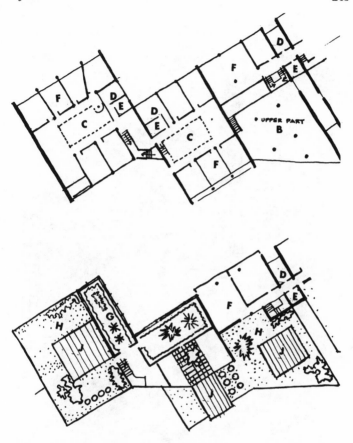

Upper floors: (B) workroom, (C) living room, (D) bath, (E) toilet, (F) private room, (G) greenhouse, (H) terrace, (J) solar collectors.

a graphics artist and printer, each with their apprentices and households (plan shown in part above).

Green Belt

Prior to the twentieth century most productive United States crop land was located at the outskirts of our cities, and even

The kitchen gardens.

as late as 1950 half such land was still to be found in and around the metropolitan areas. By 1975 farm land near cities became a rarity, agribusiness having driven out the small farmers and developers having bulldozed the farms into housing or industrial sites.

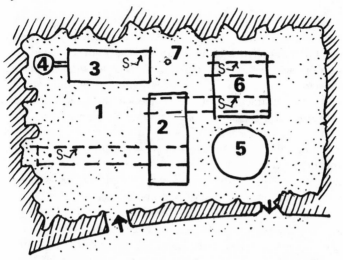

A service station on the ring road: (1) parking area, (2) agricultural implement storage, (3) kitchen for canning, dehydrating, storage, (4) smokehouse, (5) composting tanks, (6) power generator house, (7) windmill, (S) solar collectors.

In any sane view the twentieth-century despoliation of the landscape was perverse, as was the kind of planning that fostered it. To the conserving society of the twenty-first century such patterns of development appear not merely perverse but almost criminal, since they had no merit except quick money for a few at unacceptable economic and ecologic costs for the many. It was not as if no alternative scheme existed, just the opposite. As far back as the sixteenth century Elizabeth I had banned new building within three miles of London's limits, and since her time the *green belt,* as it got to be called, has been a recurrent theme in town planning.

Whether an old place is reconstructed or a new one projected, the green belt is now essential, since every town grows at least some of its food, open space for sport and recreation must be near at hand.

Although the intensively cultivated gardens of the twenty-first century with their greenhouses and fish ponds, berry patches and orchards of dwarf fruit trees, produce a good portion of each town's food, cultivating them is no backbreaking drudgery since the heavy work is lightened by the communally owned tractors and tools needed for field work, the scrubbers and pressure cookers used in the kitchens.

Along the ring road. This secondary highway is the town's trucking route. The stations are powered by waste heat from the generating plant, by windmills and solar collectors. Finally, there are landscaped areas set aside for parks and as sites for the Basic Economy settlements.

Along the through routes. Convenient to the railroad and main highway are located the extensive, mechanized farms growing grain and pulse crops, the buildings of heavy industry, a production center for Basic Economy goods, the VTOL airport. . . .

Countryside. About four miles away is the ring road of the next town. Between are meadows and woodland, streams and ponds.

Organization of a Basic Economy Production Center

The aim of the centers is to produce the required quotas of subsistence goods and maintain high quality while expending the minimum of material, energy, and time.

The goal is simple but the planning is not, for although standardization and uniformity is stressed and the goods limited to objects of basic utility, many different kinds of materials and skills enter into the making. Ore and oil must be extracted, crops grown, machines fabricated, cloth woven, food processed. . . . Each production center is designed for its use. Some are large, some small, some are in cities, some at quarries or mines, sometimes a center located in an isolated area may be the nucleus of a new town.

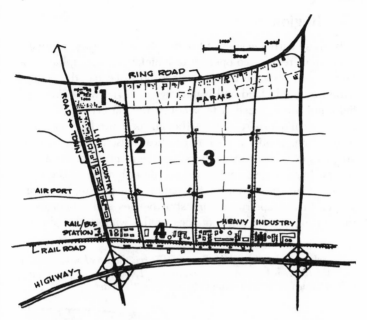

A Basic Economy production center: (1) agrobiology college and housing, (2) service centers, (3) the farm, (4) processing, storage, and shipping.

In this model the production center takes the form of a mechanized farm. The area is about three thousand acres in which are located housing and other amenities for a work force of six hundred as well as the greenhouses, shops, processing and packaging plants needed for this type of farm. In addition there are the buildings required for a small college of agrobiology.

The farming methods combine the efficiency of twentieth-century agronomy with the old (and renewed) virtues—composting, resting and replenishing the soil, converting waste and residue to useful products, avoiding pesticides.

The Region

In these early decades of the twenty-first century, mutually dependent regions co-operate to maintain demographic, economic, and ecologic balances since no place has the combination of arable land and waterways, quarries and mines, oil field and forest, needed to produce the variety of goods required in modern society. Although local products are preferred for patriotic as well as practical reasons, an active export-import exchange is an important element in the economy. As the hypothetical region we are describing is in the temperate zone, more apples are eaten than pineapples, more grapes than grapefruit, more strawberries and asparagus in the spring, prunes and potatoes in the winter, the obvious

A densely populated part of a region. Three thousand square miles with thirty townships. Average density is 1,400 persons per square mile. Highways are approximately twenty miles apart.

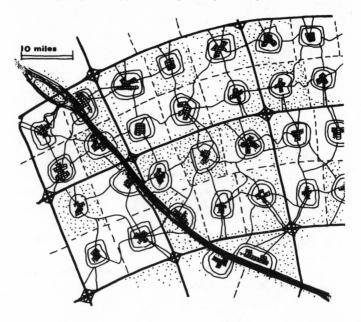

way of reducing the wasteful intermediary services of former times. But it is not merely a practical matter: An awareness of climate and season is fostered, a pride in a place and its distinctive foods and industries, its ways of doing things, and its special style in clothes and slang. This is the patriotism of the region.

World-wide, what saves modern regionalism from the curse of provincialism is good transportation routes and electronic community as well as the interpenetration of local cultures.

The Present Recalls the Past

Since nations have thrown down their arms, nationalism seems to have lost its meaning. Local flags are sprouting everywhere, all different with one exception: They all bear in no matter what language the words *co-operation, participation, responsibility*. Political boundaries having no correspondence to natural boundaries are beginning to be erased, allowing large-scale planning without artificial restraints or controls from distant capitals. In addition, some national governments have already been replaced by independent regional federations bound together by similar traditions, language, and interests. Some ask whether we are on the way to the old city-states but without walls, animosities, or class distinctions. It is possible, it could happen.

However, for me the most hopeful note is a saying recently inscribed on a new town hall. It is not from the mouth of a god or guru but from that of a modest nineteenth-century English electrician, Michael Faraday, who once said, "All this is a dream. Still, examine it by a few experiments. Nothing is too wonderful if it is consistent with the laws of nature, and in cases such as these, experiment is the best test of such consistency."

Appendices

Manhattan Island, as we here propose to alter it. Up the center of the island runs a narrow strip of business and industrial buildings, shown here by cross-hatching. On either side of it are north-and-south arterial highways. Toward both rivers are residential areas and parks, and the river banks themselves, in most parts of town, would be given over to recreation. (A) shows heliport location.

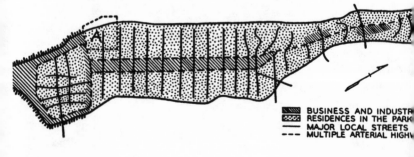

BUSINESS AND INDUSTR
RESIDENCES IN THE PARK
MAJOR LOCAL STREETS
MULTIPLE ARTERIAL HIGH

APPENDIX A[1]

A Master Plan for New York

Make no little plans; they have no magic to stir men's blood, and probably themselves will not be realized. Make big plans: aim high in hope and work, remembering that a noble, logical diagram, once recorded, will never die, but long after we are gone will be a living thing, asserting itself with ever growing insistency.—Daniel Burnham.

A Master Plan is a directive for the progressive development of a region toward its ideal form. Such a plan is possible when, without sudden and violent changes of the whole, the buildings and community functions may be gradually but systematically replaced correctly if they were not correctly placed to begin with or if their places have become outmoded. Such a plan may take two or three decades to mature, while the old structures obsolesce and the new ones are laid down in convenient order. It is worth while for such a long-range plan to aim at a high excellence.

Now the island of Manhattan can aim to be, for the next fifty years, the cultural, business, style and entertainment capital of the world. And by taking advantage, for the first time, of its rivers—hitherto almost preempted by commerce and industry—it can become a city of neighborhoods wonderful to live in, as leisurely and comfortable as it is busy and exciting. What is needed for this is a Master Plan. The majority of apartment and commercial buildings in Manhattan are now obsolescent. Therefore any proposed transformation which follows the site and which, without violence, follows the historical trends, can begin at once and be carried through in our generation. "Following historical trends" means emphasizing the location of commercial and residen-

[1] *New Republic*, Nov. 20, 1944, pp. 656–59.

tial regions as they have in fact been developing for strong natural reasons, and to regularize these trends by weeding out and zoning.

Our plan is, simply:

1. To extend the business and light industry and all through traffic of Manhattan in a continuous axis up the middle of the island.

2. To remove the through avenues on the sides and develop the land on either side of the axis in park-residential neighborhoods right down to the rivers.

3. And to develop the shores (north of, say, Twenty-third Street) as beaches for bathing, boating and promenade.

This would extend the zone of work and all through traffic in a continuous axis up the narrow island, with neighborhoods adjacent on either side, and put a stop to the tremendous twice-daily flow of uptown-downtown traffic by giving to the majority of Manhattan residents the chance of a home within walking distance of their work.

It would also clear the shores for the greater part of their 29-mile length and develop them for sport and residence, recognizing that the riverfront in Manhattan proper has diminished in commercial importance and may now be put to another use.

By making the neighborhoods more livable and using the amenities that naturally exist in this wonderful location, we can do away with the necessity of fleeing great distances for recreation, and restore leisure to a place that is notorious for its nervousness.

Historically, we may say that the first general plan of New York was the layout of the gridiron of avenues and streets around 1800, an expedient for land sale. This gridiron, with its long north-south avenues, gave to Manhattan its famous accessibility and clarity; but there is no doubt that, especially uptown, it did violence to the hillier contours; and of course it has failed to be adequate to the necessities of modern traffic.

The second plan could be considered to be the layout of the parks up the middle of the island, especially Central, Morningside and St. Nicholas Parks. This great scheme of

Randall, Vaux, Olmstead and others in the middle of the last century, and so vigilantly defended by public spirit ever since, gave the spreading city a real form; it prevented it from becoming an endless jungle of street after street. Since the rivers were given over to industry, shipping and the railroads, it at least guaranteed that some neighborhoods could face inward on a green belt. We should not for a moment venture to destroy this wonderful stratagem of the central parks, were it not the case that more and more the river-parks have proved their value and more and more the smaller parks have become the most desired neighborhoods for people who can afford them.

The third major plan, and the first Master Plan so-called, was the proposal of the City Planning Commission under Rexford Tugwell (1941), following after the unofficial New York Regional Plan of the twenties. This plan contained many subplans (for highways, sewers, health facilities, etc.), all based on the key plan showing land use. The proposed use of the land in Manhattan was a reformatory attempt to locate the industries of the island within more limited boundaries downtown and to develop them in several new belts uptown. The subplans were accepted, the key plan was rejected, and the result is that, contrary to its charter, the greatest city in the world has no Master Plan.

Manhattan Island, viewed as a whole, now exhibits the following anomalies. Ordinarily we should expect a town on an important body of water to open out toward the water for both industry and amenity; perhaps to be terraced toward it. In Manhattan, for unfortunate reasons, the people face inward, except that around much of the island there is an apartment-house cliff, so that the form of the whole is more like a bowl than a terrace. The apartments overlooking the Hudson and the East Rivers are tall because the view is desirable and the rents are high; but all others are cut off from the same amenity. Yet even the riverview dwellers have only a view but no close contact, for they are separated from the water by an obsolete railroad and an increasing number of elaborate highways.

In a deeper sense, these peripheral highways were not designed primarily for the residents of the city itself, but, like several other works of engineering of the past decade, for commuters outside the city, who choose, and can afford, to live in Westchester or on Long Island. Such means cannot solve the traffic problems of a great city! So long as 3 million people enter downtown Manhattan every day and swell the downtown population from 360,000 to nearly 4 million, and retreat again as evening falls, there will be traffic congestion and sardine-tin subways.

To build more escape-highways or new subways only invites still more people away from the center to crowd back into it during the hours of business. And vice versa, so long as the chief facilities for recreation are thrown into the periphery, at Coney Island, Van Cortland Park, Jones Beach, etc., the majority are forced to commute in the other direction and pay for a few hours of recreation with two long hours of travel.

In general, the proper solution for problems of transit is to cut down the number of trips. And this can be done only by bringing work, residence and recreation closer together. In a place like Manhattan this cannot be done by piecemeal planning; but fortunately, as we have shown, the natural site and many important historical trends, and the rapid rate of replacement, make major planning entirely feasible.

The Parts of the Physical Plan

Acreage and density. Manhattan Island is not crowded. At present it has a theoretical residential density of 200 to the acre (about 9,000 residential acres to 1,900,000 persons). And if this density fails to allow for spacious, green, livable neighborhoods, the fault lies not in the numbers but in the layout.

In the first place, correct layout would enormously increase the available residential acreage. For instance, the gridiron of streets and avenues at present uses up 27.4% of the total area of the island. By rationalizing the system of avenues into two multi-level through highways up the axis, and by closing off at least every other one of the neighborhood streets and providing for merely local neighborhood traffic, this figure could be cut in half. And if we look at the present blocks of buildings themselves—small, helter-skelter, honeycombed with vent shafts outside and with repeating stairwells inside—we can see that for the same density, a weeding out and more rational new construction would add a tremendous increment of available open space.

Let us maintain the existing density of 200 to the acre. What does this figure mean in terms of living? It is certainly not a place of private houses and little gardens (45 to the acre); but Manhattanites do not require these in any case; for those who choose the cosmopolitan way of life are manning, and supporting by their rent, a center of world culture and world affairs, and they enjoy the advantages and monuments of such a center. Yet it is a place where, if people lived in tall buildings (15 stories), every room would face on a Madison or Washington Square; and where, if they lived in a combination of tall and low buildings (three stories) on every other street, there would be room for a football field!

The zone of industry and commerce. The economy of Manhattan comprises: the light manufacture of consumers' goods and small machined parts; shipping and moderately heavy warehousing; business management and finance; retailing and display; ideas, styles, entertainment. It is an economy of relatively small shops whose materials are brought and whose products are carted away by truck. There is no heavy industry to speak of. During peacetime the volume of heavy shipping was sharply falling off, and the war has shown that the present docks are three or four times too large for peacetime demands.

Nothing therefore stands in the way of extending this economy up the entire island. Already in the Tugwell plan, following the actual trends, isolated new commercial districts were recommended uptown. We propose simply to unite these in a continuous belt served by continuous highways and to relocate uptown not only business but places of light manufacture (e.g., the garment industry). But the advantages of doing this are extraordinary; for it means that many hundreds of thousands of workers, instead of traveling the whole length of the island twice a day, could now live in the neighborhoods next to their work.

Up and down this great Main Street, the different kinds

of industry would find their own zones. It is reasonable to assume that Midtown, the site of the great terminals and therefore of the great hotels, would continue to be the entertainment, style and idea center; and that business and finance would cluster in its cliffs around Wall Street. The ships and warehouses must occupy the downtown shores. (Therefore we provide in Greenwich Village a downtown residential neighborhood in the center rather than on the shore.) But the great mass of business and manufacture that now sporadically mars the whole breadth of Manhattan could find its place anywhere from north to south between the highways.

Airport. To provide for air transport, of persons and commodities, is perhaps the thorniest problem in all cosmopolitan planning. No existent city is adapted for the large landing fields and the noise of an airport. The expedient up to now has been to locate the airport on the outskirts—requiring an hour's travel for a trip that itself may last only an hour. The airport must somehow be brought near the center. But the rapid evolution of air technique makes it again difficult to know what kind and how large a space can be allotted. A number of modern plans provide for helicopter landings on the roofs of large buildings.

As a tentative proposal, we have chosen an area on the Hudson River from Forty-second to Twenty-third Streets. The river provides an open space for maneuvering. Immediately accessible on one side is the midtown section of the terminals and hotels; and on the other side the zone of shipping and warehousing. The airport itself is conceived as the roof of an enormous warehouse shed.

Residential neighborhoods and the use of the rivers. We come now to the residential neighborhoods themselves, extending on either side of the axis right down to the Hudson, East and Harlem Rivers; served by regular cross highways to the main highways, but without any through traffic.

These neighborhoods must be thought of not as places accessible to parks, but as parks in themselves—for the formal parks of Manhattan are being sacrificed to them. As our discussion of density has shown, it is not important whether the houses are high or low; obviously there should be a combination of both. But their layout must be such as to be in a park, and, where possible, to face toward the water, to be terraced toward the water. The rivers, the park and the habitations must be a continuous visual and ambulatory experience. The urban park must not be a place of escape but a place in which to live.

It is to be hoped that such neighborhoods, where people feel they live rather than merely sleep, would develop sharp local peculiarities. For instance (if we may propose something that will make many people's hair stand on end), let certain great masterpieces of art be decentralized from the Metropolitan Museum of Art and placed in neighborhood post offices and churches, or a world-famous statue on a fountain; then the neighbors might get to live with these in a rather closer way, and art lovers have to seek them out in parts of our city that they would otherwise never visit.

Except for a few spots where the currents are dangerous, Manhattan's rivers are ideal for swimming and boating. (The job of cleaning them up has already begun and is on the postwar agenda.) Let them finally be used by everybody, as they are now by the venturesome boys. Visitors to Chicago or Rio, for instance, know what it means to have a great sweep of water for bathing at the foot of every street, and Manhattan has twice and three times as much shorefront per person.

To make a bathing resort of residential Manhattan Island is a grandiose project; but it is not nearly so grandiose as for tens of thousands to go off on every hot day to places 10 to 50 miles away from their homes.

The idea of Manhattan. This plan for Manhattan Island is not a plan for the New York region. Most often, to make such an isolated plan is ruinous; but Manhattan has a peculiar role not only in the New York region but in the world (which is the true region of our cosmopolis). Its problems, and its advantages, are not those of its surroundings.

In general, the great urban communities of America would be better if they were smaller in size; if they had a closer and less parasitic dependence on the surrounding agriculture; if their manufacturers sprang more directly from their regional resources. This rule, we say, applies to other cities. Yet there is no need to defend Manhattan Island; she has her own rule; there is no need to praise her, though we who are her sons are often betrayed into doing so. She has long been the capital not of a region but of a nation; and it is curious that this came about. For it was as a center through which produce passed and was processed that New York first became great. Yet now the material shipments more and more go elsewhere, and the manufacturers are only light manufacturers; but Manhattan is greater still. Within ten years she has become the intellectual and artistic capital of the world—for all Europe has come here. She is the foster-parent of lasting ideas and temporary fashions; of entertainments and of industrial plans that often go elsewhere to get their tangible body, but their spirit has something in it of Manhattan. That is, of the seaport and its mixed races, and the politically subtle workers in light industry, the mass-entertainers and the free artists.

Surely we people of Manhattan do not set as our ideal (if we could afford it) to live in a suburb. But to live as a matter of course in our own place, the most elegant and unhurried on earth.

Feasibility

This plan is physically, economically and socially feasible and advantageous.

1. In the interest of the shore neighborhoods, we diminish the waterfront available for shipping and remove the Hudson River tracks. But the tracks have long been moribund, and peacetime shipping is progressively being reduced.

2. Important progress toward the completion of the plan could begin immediately after the war (as part of the billion-dollar six-year budget). It is estimated that from 75 to 80% of the buildings in Manhattan are overage and there will be vast reconstruction on any plan whatsoever. But the city's largest and newest buildings do fall in the zones here proposed (e.g., Rockefeller Center, the Empire State Building, the downtown skyscrapers, the great hotels, etc.).

3. The giving up of the parks in the central axis provides an enormous reservoir of land to exchange for the commer-

cial and industrial property now located along the rivers, the sites of the future residential parks. As these business sites progressively obsolesce and are condemned, space can be allotted to them in the large buildings in the main axis; therefore the transition can be made with a minimum of hardship. Further, the money value of a square foot of land along the central Main Street would be at least five times that in the scattered sites to be condemned; and this would provide a great fund to carry out the plan. The amount of land available for exchange in the new Main Street zone comes close to 1500 acres, valued at business center prices.

4. "If it were possible to translate into dollars the time consumed by workers in excess travel, the result would be startling. At least one million persons spend two hours a day going to and from work in New York. At 50 cents an hour, this becomes a million dollars a day or $312 million a year. This is three percent of $10 billion, which would pay for rebuilding large sections of New York City without calculating revenues from rents."—Cleveland Rogers.

5. The political and legal opposition to this plan is the same as that to any other Master Plan. Long-range and large-scale zoning involves the destruction of speculation in land values. Those who rely for their profits not on rents but on speculation, have contrived to veto even the modest proposals of the Tugwell plan. But it seems to us that the proposal here made is at once so arresting and so simple, so grounded in the site and the history of the city and in the experience of its citizens, that it can arouse the public enthusiasm necessary to overcome this opposition, and end the anomaly of the greatest city in the world having no Master Plan at all.

APPENDIX B

Improvement of Fifth Avenue

As early as 1870, it was proposed, by Egbert L. Viele and others, to double-deck Lower Broadway and Wall Street because of "excessive and dangerous congestion." We here make a similar proposal to revive the amenity of New York's great shopping and promenade street, Fifth Avenue.

The present ground level is widened by the elimination of the sidewalks and all pedestrian use.

Sixteen feet above it we would construct a continuous promenade from 34th Street to 59th Street. This mall is accessible by ramps and stairways from the side streets, and provided with a slow moving shoppers' trolley of its own.

The new Fifth Avenue is treated as a street of fountains, arcades, sidewalk cafes, elegant shops, and interesting vistas; the place, as at present, for public ceremonies, parades, and celebrations, that can now be unhurried and not disrupt the city's traffic.

As a further proposal, the entire area from 8th Avenue to 3rd Avenue could be similarly double-decked.

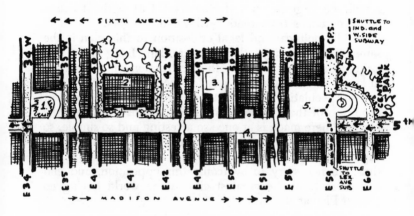

Plan for double decking 5th Avenue from 34th St. to 59th St. 1. Ramp with new office buildings over 2. Public library 3. Rockefeller Center 4. St. Patrick's Cathedral 5. Grand Army Plaza. Below is shuttle to East and West Side subways.

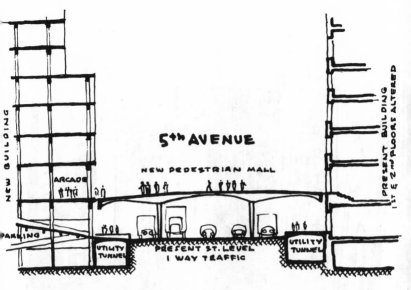

5th AVENUE

NEW PEDESTRIAN MALL

NEW BUILDING

ARCADE

PARKING

UTILITY TUNNEL

PRESENT ST. LEVEL
1 WAY TRAFFIC

UTILITY TUNNEL

PRESENT BUILDING
1ST & 2ND FLOORS ALTERED

Section through Fifth Ave.

*Grand Army Plaza
at 60th St. looking south*

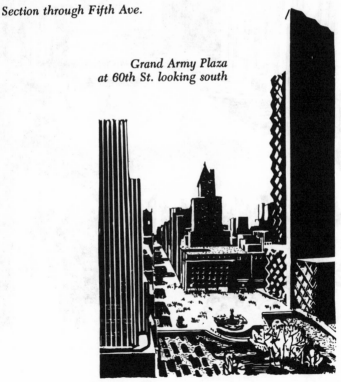

On St. Patrick's Day

Looking north from 47th St.
The pools in the foreground are on wheels.

The public library

APPENDIX C

Housing in New York City

In New York City the housing problem is more difficult than elsewhere. There is too much substandard housing, not enough housing altogether, standard or substandard, and not enough space to build new housing before demolishing old, so there is the headache of relocation during the interims. (There are 280,000 substandard units. The estimated need for total housing is 65,000 a year, the net new building is 16,000.)

Now in charge of building and financing such housing are many agencies, some designed for housing the poor, some for housing generally, some agents of the city, but others agents of the State and Federal governments. They are, in part, the Housing Authority, the Mayor's Commission on Slum Clearance and Urban Renewal, the Comptroller's Office, the Board of Estimate, the Bureau of Real Estate, the Department of Buildings, and various State and Federal

Housing Agencies. Meantime, uncoordinated with these, there are agencies in charge of location of schools (Board of Education), and playgrounds and parks (Parks). Transportation by rail falls to the Transit Authority, but if it is automotive it may fall to the Port Authority (for certain highways, tunnels, and bridges) or the Triborough Bridge and Tunnel Authority (for other highways, etc.). When cars are moving or parked in the streets, they belong to the Traffic Department; and safety in general belongs to the Police. Nobody as such attends to the specific relation of workers and their particular industries, the cause of all this commutation, but there are zoning laws for broad kinds of occupancy, under the City Planning Commission. Neighborhood quarrels, family disruption, etc., might be handled by the Police and various Social agencies. Other departments, too, have a hand in the community planning of New York, e.g., Public Works, Gas, Water and Electricity, etc.

This is not very promising. Further, it is generally agreed that unaided private enterprise cannot fill three-fourths of the housing need. It is agreed that income-segregation has undesirable effects, is a condition of juvenile delinquency, unsafe streets. Racial segregation is a problem not beginning to be solved. The traffic congestion is intolerable.

Under the circumstances it seems reasonable to ask if the *integration* of all these various functions is not relevant? To give a partial list: housing, slum-clearance, location of industries, transportation, adequate schools and teachers, clean streets, traffic control, social work, racial harmony, master planning, recreation. The list could be long extended, not to speak of a convenient and beautiful city and local patriotism. It is not to be hoped that in the near future we can have an efficient, viable, peaceful city. But we do have the right to demand that the manifold functions (and their problems) be regarded in an overall view as functions of one community. Apart from such a unified view, the apparent solution of this or that isolated problem *inevitably* leads to disruption elsewhere. Escape thoroughfares must aggravate central traffic. Slum-clearance as an isolated policy must aggravate class stratification. New subways aggravate conurbation. "Housing" makes for double shift and overcrowded classrooms. No Master Plan guarantees foolishness like the Lincoln Square project. These consequent evils then produce new evils among them. Isolated planning *cannot* make sense. Therefore we propose a Community Planning Agency.

Such a body would at least coordinate. But it should also know how to draw out and explain the bearings and the effects of isolated actions and proposals, for even the best-intentioned actions in such a social area as physical planning often have far-reaching disastrous effects that the planners never thought of. (At present, the likely undesirable social effects of physical proposals come to light, if at all, only by the clamor of *ad hoc* pressure groups of citizens who foresee where the shoe will pinch. The protest is bound to be weak, and it has no competent body to appeal to. Usually it is disregarded, and once a thing is built it's built and stays.) On the other hand, there are plans of multi-valued community benefit which require the cooperation of several departments, but which are not immediately relevant enough to any one to get sponsorship. These would be precisely appropriate to a Community Planning Agency. It would have community suggestions, ideals, and proposals of its own. It could set before the citizens reasonably integrated pictures of what various plans and policies concretely mean in each one's way of life, so that choices—e.g., referenda on financing public works—can be made not completely in the dark. And the Agency would propose its own programs.

2

Isolated approaches can always have routine plans to fit narrow programs. Broadly conceived approaches, that try to cope with the complex reality, have no such wisdom. They must proceed variously and experimentally and find which hypotheses confirm themselves in action. It is not even sufficient to find out what people want and give them that, for, as Catherine Bauer put it, "We can only want what we know. Deeper analysis may suggest some entirely novel arrangement. The only way such an arrangement can be tested is by experimentation with its actual use, not by asking opinions in advance." So the community approach must be not only varied and experimental but inventive.

What warrants the uniformity of plans of the Housing Authority? As we pointed out in the text above (p. 53) the standards fit the customs of neither the tenants nor the designers. They are sociological abstractions of an "American Standard" with little imagination of the actual residents. Space is sacrificed for building services and domestic appliances. Poor tenants arrive and do not find room for the little furniture they have. Are the larger cold-water railroad flats in the same neighborhood, at a cheaper rental, *necessarily* less desirable? Not much use is made of sharing appliances as a way to save expense. Spaces are uniformly partitioned in a very few categories, though specific occupants might have quite different needs. (E.g., in Sweden a spacious common room is much wanted.) Given a minimum budget, is the standard bathroom a minimum? In certain Swedish plans—we cite them because the Swedes are thought to have a quality standard higher than ours—the bathroom is a toilet seat with a shower directly above it; hands are washed in the kitchen sink. In a development in Leipzig, tenants wanted balconies, and central heating was not considered an equal value.

(If the reader will thumb through such a volume as Elizabeth Denby's *Europe Rehoused,* he will get no uniform impression of what people consider fundamentally essential.)

Plaster and paint are considered a minimum amenity, despite the cost of upkeep; tile would not do. Yet a few years ago in this same city, wall-paper was an indispensable amenity. Is it always wise to spend money to landscape an insufficient space?

We need not mention the pointlessness of repeating the same elevation in a dozen buildings, because this is not policy but timidity and laziness. Though indeed, as came out in the recent public attacks on some small attempts to beautify new school buildings, there is a widespread feeling that variety and unconventional shapes and colors *must* be wasteful and are certainly wicked.

3

On the other hand, if we take a community approach instead of a "houser's" approach, we might have thoughts like the following. Perhaps variety of occupancy makes for the best neighborhood. Certainly income-segregation is unfortunate. How can we get more types together? Might not the exclusive barrier between public and private financing be broken down and various other arrangements be tried?

Hudson Guild conducted a brilliant project in the Chelsea district, getting a few Puerto Rican families to take pride in their flats by building furniture, repairing, and decorating, under expert guidance. There is a lesson here. Use the people of the community-block instead of other paid labor. Youth for janitoring, grounds, and landscaping, as collegians work for their keep. Perhaps the very apartment spaces could be left more open, for the tenants to decide on their own partitioning and help build it. Artistic effects are possible: the modern Mexicans have paved their walks with mosaics of colored stones and broken bath-tiles, rather than black asphalt, because they have had willing labor.

True, if you give people the sense that they can make and change things, there might be a little constructive demolition to remedy what the architect did wrong. These are the risks one takes.

Such activities require leadership. Have efforts been made to get community leadership right into the neighborhood block? For there is plenty of leadership, paid and voluntary, in the social agencies and settlement houses. Might not leaders, ministers, teachers, even politicians, be encouraged by better quarters to live in the place and take some responsibility for it? Consider racial integration: has enough attempt been made at invited racial integration?

There are always too many applicants. ("More than 250,-000 families applied for admission to the 17,040 apartments made avaliable by the Authority during 1943–44.") Perhaps mutual community utility could be a major principle of selection. We recall the arrangement common in Paris after

Hausmann rebuilt it: there was a shop on the first floor, the poor family inhabited the mansard, and the rich and middle class occupied the remainder.

APPENDIX D[1]

A Plan for the Rejuvenation of a Blighted Industrial Area in New York City (1944–45)

The present plight of Long Island City is by no means exclusive to New York. Most of America's metropolitan centers have one or more sections suffering from similar obolescence and blight. Flanked by the East River and Manhattan Island on the west and the borough of Queens on the east, Long Island City was nevertheless completely overlooked during the flagrant exploitation of Queens during the early part of the century and has been ever since. It was already partially built up when suburban development reached its heyday and eager speculators passed it up for fresh, unimproved land beyond. Even by 1910, it had a clearcut industrial character and was later zoned for such use—a measure which unfortunately discouraged residential building and left a myriad of small parcels of vacant land spotted at random between existing factories. Since 1915 three subways and numerous surface transportation lines have been built through the area to make connections between Manhattan and Queens, but still it has reaped little or no improvement from its new-found strategic location. Further in its favor as a convenient residential section is the Queensboro Bridge approach located at its very core and the Queens-Midtown tunnel at its low extremity.

[1] Description of project by the editors of the *Architectural Forum,* February, 1946.

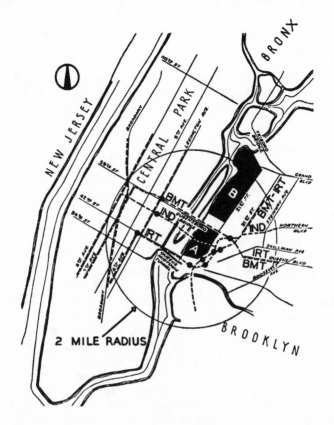

Showing proximity to the city center, convenience of transportation, and riverside location. To the south is the "Riverview" residential community (A); to the north, the "work residence" community (B).

Despite its location (fifteen minutes of easy travel to Times Square), and good transportation facilities, Long Island City's present condition is one of advanced decay. Though the huge Sunnyside freight and the passenger yards belonging to the Pennsylvania Railroad inject some life and small commerce, their inland site has tended to draw building and development away from the waterfront, while the existence of two car-float terminals from Staten Island and New Jersey has rendered the riverfront anything but desirable for residence. As a result vacant land abounds; values are low, ranging from 50 cents to $2.25 per sq. ft. and lowest near the shoreline. According to the 1930 census, Long Island City's population was only 40,800, representing a density of about 23 persons per acre. What dwellings exist, are, for the most part, slums or near-slums, having been built prior to 1899.

Because of its size and proximity to midtown New York, it is only logical that such an area should be a healthy, active and important part of greater New York and not the liability that its delinquent taxes and low values represent today. With this in mind two schemes of redevelopment are proposed. 1. A community, zoning existing light manufacturing and residence extending from Hallets Cove to the Queensbridge Houses north of Queensboro Bridge. This project was designed by the City Planning Group of Columbia University under the direction of Percival Goodman. 2. South of the bridge extending to 35th Street is the proposed 114 acre Riverview Community designed by Pomerance and Breines, Andrew J. Thomas and Percival Goodman, Associated Architects. This project takes full advantage of a waterfront location and the striking skyline view offered by Manhattan's tall buildings across the river. It is intended to house some 50,000 persons (because of present low density, this would call for rehousing only about 5,000). Privately financed and paying full taxes, it is estimated that rents would run between $11.50 and $25.00 per room per month. The project, which encompasses about one-quarter of the total area, is bounded to the North by the Queensboro Bridge approach and the existing Queensbridge housing project. Further north, and also on the river, is planned another residential section with a density of about 200 persons per acre. Between the latter and the Sunnyside yards to the east would be located a third neighborhood zoned for housing and restricted industry. The planners foresee that many existing non-nuisance factories could be retained in this area and converted into local assets rather than liabilities. They feel that the existing street pattern should not be altered but merely blocked at given points to increase land values and improve the appearance of the community as a whole.

Naturally, such a plan calls for rezoning of the "work-residence" type with its obvious advantages: lower transportation costs for the worker who can live near his place of employment, a rise in land values in the sections now overzoned for industry, replacement of industrial slums with parks, playgrounds and other public conveniences. Also included in the plan is provision for the improvement of existing overhead transportation structures and replanning of through traffic at Queens Plaza, a nearby intersection and passenger transfer point of intense congestion.

DISCARDED

ADIRONDACK COMMUNITY COLLEGE
LIBRARY DISCARDED